STOCK BROTH & BOWL

OTHER BOOKS BY
JONATHAN BENDER

Cookies & Beer
LEGO: A Love Story

//

To my mom, who makes chicken soup that cures all ills.
And to my grandmother, the only woman who could ever
get me to eat creamed mushroom soup out of a can.

//

STOCK BROTH & BOWL

RECIPES FOR COOKING, DRINKING & NOURISHING

Jonathan Bender

Photography by Ben Pieper

Andrews McMeel Publishing®

Kansas City · Sydney · London

Contents

Introduction

Stock is the little black dress of your fridge.

It can be sexy, but it's more likely to be sensible. It's great on its own, but it is, by nature, unfinished. Think of it as a perfect start. It gives you the base that you can then accessorize or build on to make that killer outfit, which, in this case, is a righteous cup of drinking broth or a dinner that sparkles because it starts with the stock you're about to learn how to make.

Stock shouldn't be a convenience food—it takes time to develop flavor. But that doesn't mean it can't make your life more convenient. Stock and broth are being touted as miracle cures. And they are miracle cures . . . for your meal plan.

Stock, Broth & Bowl is about investing time and effort in the beginning of the week to help you eat well the *entire* week. I'm breaking down stock to its base elements, giving you options—whether it is made with animal bones, root vegetables, or shrimp shells because the versatility of stock is its true beauty.

The nine stocks in this book intentionally build in complexity from straightforward bone-based creations to spiced and sweet pots of liquid great for drinking or braising. Chefs Alex Pope and Todd Schulte, who own a butcher shop and a soup company respectively, developed the stock recipes. That's because outside of grandmas, butchers and soup makers are the people who best know what to do with bones and stock.

The stock recipes are also right-sized. The goal is to let you produce enough, 2 to 3 quarts, to have a few cups of drinking broth during a week, as well as make the one or two recipes provided for each stock. I don't want this to be a flash in the flavor pan for you. Let's treat this like a summer camp romance: Fall in love with something new every week, and if it turns out you want to keep writing after you get home from camp, you can easily double what's recommended and store your extra stock in the freezer.

The first way the stocks become finished broths is through an infusion of herbs or aromatics. This gives you something to sip while you think about what you want to cook for the upcoming week. I'll share three suggestions for each stock, but my hope is that you'll take these as suggestions, not gospel. Broths are best treated like taco bars and frozen yogurt shops—cram them full of what you love and just try not to put together too many flavors that conflict (read: gummy bears and anything else).

The lunch, dinner, and side recipes that follow are designed to show off the time you spent building flavor in stock. The Braised Short Ribs (page 46) are straightforward to prepare but have spice and brightness because of the Orange & Guajillo Chile Turkey Stock (page 43). There's also a host of one-pot meals like the Ancho Chile Chicken Tacos (page 29), which follow the same path as the stock—a little bit of prep and a lot of unattended cooking time in exchange for an Instagram-worthy dish.

Stock has long been a part of what makes food delicious. And now broth, its finished, seasoned counterpart, is finally getting some of the same heat. On a cool fall day, I had a cup of The Roots Stock infused with lemongrass (page xviii) and a Pig Man on Campus (page 34) cocktail later in the afternoon. The flavors weren't the revelation. The revelation was the idea that broth can be so easily integrated into my diet in meaningful and tasty ways.

This is about being realistic about the time you can commit to making stock or preparing drinking broth. You're not opening up a soup shop, but you can make a soup that makes friends think you should. You are not a pot watcher. You don't want to stand over a stove for hours on end, moving a wooden spoon in slow, mindless circles. You're a human being with a dog to walk, a toddler to chase, or a DVR list that's not getting any shorter.

Being busy is what made it easy to accept the wrongful notion that stock is a food that takes too much effort in the modern era. The truth is that stock is exactly what you need today. It's what lets you create drinking broths and layers of flavor in a midweek dinner that you've got to make after you get home from work. It's time to *Stock, Broth & Bowl*.

A Well-Stocked Kitchen

EQUIPMENT

Stockpot. If you don't own one, borrow one the first time you make stock. Some are oval-shaped, and some are taller. Some are made of thin metal. We're taking a cue from Goldilocks here on size and fit. I have short arms—using the tallest stockpots on the market are like being in Cirque du Soleil for me.

If you want to take the plunge, follow the example of a friend's husband during the wedding-registry process: He sat at tables and imagined eating cereal from each of the potential bowls on their registry. Stand over a pot in an aisle and imagine adding ingredients, and more importantly, emptying them without the hot metal touching your arms or chest. A 12-quart stockpot with straight sides will give you plenty of room (and the opportunity to double the recipes in this book if you want to make a big old batch of stock). As far as material, stainless steel with an aluminum core in the base is a good mid-point option, price wise, and will also heat rapidly and evenly.

Dutch Oven. It took a few years of marriage before my wife and I learned that if you bid on items in a silent auction, there's a good chance you might be taking them home. (We still have a significant collection of artist-painted children's chairs, if anyone's interested.) But one of the auction items that we purchased as newlyweds was a 5½-quart enamel cast iron Dutch oven.

I never knew how much I could love a given pot. A Dutch oven is ovenproof, so you can sear a steak on a burner and then finish it in the oven. It's why I don't fire up my grill in the winter, which is sacrilege in Kansas City. I also recommend using it often in the

recipes that follow for a reason: One-pot cooking, whether you live alone or with someone else, is the bee's knees. Less cleaning, particularly after a hearty meal, is always a welcome prospect.

Slow Cooker. I understand that cooking something on my stove for 24 hours is safe. I understand the same can be said of bungee jumping. I have no real desire to test either theory. A slow cooker solves my internal dilemma. The only recipe in this book that requires 24 hours is the one for Bone Broth (page 38), and it's a cakewalk in a slow cooker. Treat this purchase like a rice cooker: Find one that is clean and cheap at a garage sale. People are (wrongly) giving up on these beauties all the time. Keep in mind, you'll need a slow cooker with at least a 6- to 7-quart capacity.

Slotted Spoon. A slotted spoon lets you take out solids from your stock while retaining as much of the liquid as possible.

Coffee Filters (#6 if you see them). Our children may not know what a traditional drip coffeemaker looks like (their destiny appears to be that of the cordless phone), but coffee filters still have plenty of utility. They're functional and sturdy and perfectly suited for straining.

Fine-Mesh Strainer/Colander. The filters mean that you can use either a strainer or colander for straining. Opt for a bigger diameter—you want a wide target for when you're pouring out your stock—and very fine holes.

Pot Holders. Your stockpot will get hot on the stove. You want heavy-duty pot holders because you're going to be holding that stockpot for a while.

French Press. This is a great way to steep hot stock and infuse it with aromatics or herbs for drinking. It's got a built-in strainer, so you're not picking pieces of ginger out of your teeth, and they're built to hold hot liquids.

INGREDIENT SOURCES

When it comes to sourcing bones, you have to decide whether the animal's diet matters to you. If you're looking for bones from grass-fed cattle, you can order them online, look for a family farm at a farmers' market, or find them at a whole animal butcher.

Butcher shops and meat markets are good places to start—anywhere where they actually cut meat. Asian and Mexican markets will also help with your grocery list.

As for the types of bones that work in stock, ask your butcher for "meaty bones." If you tell him what it is you're making, he'll likely steer you toward leg bones, rib bones, neck bones (typically the cheapest option), and marrow bones. At some grocery stores, like Whole Foods, these come mixed together in a bag found in the freezer section.

By asking for "meaty bones," too, you'll also give the butcher enough leeway that he or she can supply you what's on hand, often for far less than what the frozen bag or packaged collection of bones costs.

For chickens and turkeys, the easiest place to find the bones is to start with a bone-in breast or whole bird. Outside of Thanksgiving, that might be your best bet if you're looking to make turkey stock. If you're not comfortable roasting a whole chicken, you can salvage the carcass from a grocery store rotisserie chicken.

Butchers often have chicken necks and wings—they just won't be on display. You can even store breast, wing, or thigh bones in the freezer. Simply wrap in foil and then store in a freezer bag until you're ready to make stock.

As for shrimp shells, save dinner castoffs or ask the guy working the fish counter nicely (if they have preshelled shrimp) if he happens to have some shells in back.

A NOTE ON ROASTING BONES

Some stocks made with bones will have you roast the bones before you put them in the pot. The recipes in this book don't include that step because we're aiming for more versatile base stocks that you can turn into a lot of different dishes. When you roast the bones, the stocks will have a meatier flavor and darker appearance. This is about the intensity of flavor, similar to dark versus light roasts of coffee. We're striving for something more delicate that you can then build on to drink or cook.

TECHNIQUES
Straining

When it comes to making stock, everyone has a different tip for straining. I simply go by what I have on hand at the moment and the clarity of stock I want.

You're going to have to filter the stock twice. The first time, you'll want to ladle out the stock into a mesh strainer or colander over a large metal bowl or pot. If you pour the stock over the bones or remove the bones, you'll have cloudier stock.

For the second pass, I line the fine-mesh strainer with a slightly wet coffee filter (#6 are a bit bigger and give you more area to pour into) and place a large metal bowl beneath it. The stock will flow through the filter easier if it's a bit wet. Coffee filters are as effective as cheesecloth and less expensive. Although if there's cheesecloth in your kitchen, go ahead and use it. Both will catch the solids and oil/fat from the stock.

If you discover that stock is your thing and you're doing this every weekend, then you might want to consider investing in an 8- or 10-inch bouillon strainer. They've got a long handle, with a deep basket for holding bones, and many of them can be cleaned in the dishwasher.

Cooling

After you've strained the stock, it needs to be cooled. If you place a hot pot or the bowl in the refrigerator, it won't cool fast enough to be safe. A better prospect is to create an ice bath in your sink. Fill your sink with cold water and ice and submerge the metal container with stock in the ice bath. Stir the stock every 15 minutes to help release heat. At the same time, you can drain some water and add more ice. Once your food is 40°F, it's safe to place the bowl or pot of stock in your fridge.

Clarifying Stock

If you're going to be drinking the broth or simply prefer liquid that's not cloudy, you can clarify your stock. Follow the straining steps (as outlined on page xiv) until the moment you add the container of stock to an ice bath. Instead pour the strained stock into a straight-sided pot over medium-high heat. In a small mixing bowl, place 2 large egg whites (discard the yolks), 2 tablespoons of water, and ½ tablespoon of lemon juice. Whip until frothy, about 30 seconds.

Add the egg mixture to the pot while the stock is simmering and stir gently with a whisk to keep the egg whites from sticking to the bottom. The egg whites, along with the small particulates in your stock, will begin to float to the surface. Stop stirring and allow the raft (the name given to the collection of solids) to form. You can let the stock come to a simmer but not a boil. After 20 minutes, strain the stock through a coffee filter again into a bowl or pot. Immerse in an ice bath. When cooled, portion it out by cup or quart and place in the refrigerator.

You can also clarify stock after it has been refrigerated. It's nice because a lot of the fat will have risen to form a cap on top of the stock, which can then be easily removed. In that case, you'd simply place a quart of stock (after removing that cap) in a small saucepan over medium heat. When it's lukewarm, add the egg white mixture to the stock over medium heat. Bring the stock to a simmer. Stir it gently to keep the egg whites from sticking to the bottom of the pot, but once it begins forming the raft, leave it alone for 20 minutes. Then strain the stock through a coffee filter or cheesecloth. You can use the back of a spoon to keep the raft in the pot, but it doesn't matter if it falls into the strainer.

Storing

Stock will keep in an airtight container in the refrigerator for 2 to 4 days. If you leave the fat cap that forms on the top of the stock, it may keep longer.

There's a chance you might use all of the broth you make in a given weekend, but the odds are better that you're going to be freezing some. Here are a few different containers that will work and give you some options for drinking or eating.

Ice Cube Trays: Ice cube trays hold roughly 2 tablespoons (⅛ cup) of stock in each well. After the stock has frozen (6 to 12 hours), you can pop out the cubes into a freezer-safe bag and then portion accordingly.

Yogurt Containers: The type with actual lids, not foil-wrapped, are good for holding 1 cup of stock. Leave some space, at least ½ inch, for the stock to expand when it freezes.

Silicone Molds: You probably already have some in your house. But it turns out the things you've been using to make cupcakes are great for storing stock. Slide a half baking sheet or piece of cardboard under the molds so they don't spill while the stock is freezing (6 to 12 hours). If you don't know how much the mold holds, fill a measuring cup with water and fill one of the molds and then you know.

Quart-Size Jars: You can use glass or plastic jars. Each quart-size jar will hold a little under 4 cups, as you want to leave about an inch of space to allow the liquid to expand in the freezer.

Thawing Frozen Stock

If you remember, you can thaw your stock by moving it to the refrigerator 24 hours before you need it to cook.

If you've used a plastic container to store the stock, run warm water over the sides of the container in the sink. Gently squeeze the sides of the container to loosen the stock. Once it's loose enough to slide out, you can then place the stock in a pot on medium heat to defrost.

You can defrost stock stored in glass jars by steaming. Place 2 inches of water in a medium pot and bring to a boil. Place a steaming basket on top of the pot and place the glass jar in the basket. After about 30 minutes, the stock will be thawed. Handle the glass carefully with pot holders, as it will be very hot to the touch.

The Roots Stock

Alex Pope, Kansas City, Missouri

Makes 2 to 2½ quarts

1 fennel bulb

1 celery root

4 large carrots

4 large parsnips

1 large yellow onion

¼ cup vegetable oil

2 tablespoons kosher salt

3 quarts (12 cups) cold water

2 tablespoons apple cider vinegar

12 sprigs (¾ ounce) fresh oregano

Bright and light, this stock shows you why chefs sing the praises of roasting root vegetables. The carrots, onion, and celery root lend a comforting sweetness while the fennel gives off the enticing aroma of licorice as you're in the kitchen. The clean freshness of this stock means you'll be sneaking a sip while you strain just as you can't resist licking the bowl when you're making cookies.

///

Preheat the oven to 450°F. Trim the stalks off the fennel bulb—you can eat the fronds in a salad or discard—and chop the stalks into 1-inch pieces. Trim the bottom of the bulb to remove any part of the root and then slice the bulb in half vertically. Give it one more horizontal cut and then chop into 1-inch pieces. Place the fennel in a medium-size bowl.

Rinse the celery root and chop off the base where the roots meet the body. Then chop it, along with the carrots, parsnips, and onion, into 1-inch pieces. Add all four to the bowl with the fennel and then toss with the vegetable oil and salt until evenly coated. Place the vegetables on a baking sheet in an even single layer and bake for 15 minutes, until the edges are browned but not burnt.

Place the vegetables and the oil drippings in a large stockpot. Add the water, vinegar, and oregano. Turn the heat to medium-high

Once bubbles break the surface, about 20 minutes, turn the heat down to medium-low. You never want the stock to reach a roiling boil; instead keep it at a steady simmer for 2 hours. If it doesn't boil, there's nothing to skim away. You're shooting for about a bubble per second and no more than 4 bubbles per second.

Remove the stockpot from the heat. Place a large metal bowl or pot beneath a fine-mesh strainer or colander and ladle in the stock. You're going to strain the stock again. Line the strainer with a slightly damp coffee filter (#6) and add the stock. After the second pass, fill your sink with cold water and ice and submerge the metal container with stock in the ice bath. Stir the stock every 15 minutes to help release heat. At the same time, you can drain some water and add more ice. Once your food is 40°F, it's safe to place the bowl or pot of stock in your fridge.

Store in an airtight container for 2 to 4 days. If you want to freeze the stock, pour it into a freezer-safe container with the lid off. Leave ½ inch to 1 inch of space to allow for the stock to expand. After 6 hours in the freezer, place the lid on your stock and label it with the date it's frozen. You'll want to use it within 4 months.

TO ENJOY AS A DRINKING BROTH: Pour 1 cup of hot stock into a mug or French press. Add a sprig of oregano and steep for 10 minutes. Remove the oregano. Salt to taste. If you want a bit of heat, you can add a few drops of chili oil. You could also try star anise seeds if you love the distinctive taste of licorice.

NOTE: Fennel is available year-round, but it's best in late fall to early spring. When picking a fennel bulb, look for one that is white and green with no brown spots. You want the bulb to have tightly packed layers and firm stalks.

Perfect Green Hummus

Serves 6 to 8

2 (15-ounce) cans garbanzo beans (3 cups)

1 cup The Roots Stock (page xviii)

¼ cup freshly squeezed lemon juice

1 green onion, minced

1 clove garlic, minced

1 cup fresh cilantro, finely chopped

½ cup fresh Italian parsley, finely chopped

½ tablespoon curry powder

Kosher salt and freshly ground pepper

Carrot sticks, for serving

Hummus suffers from an unfair reputation because of the chalky, gritty tubs that sit wisely untouched at parties and picnics. This is like Olivia Pope rehabilitated hummus—it's light and fresh. The herbs pick up the sweetness from The Roots Stock, and the curry in the finish means the smooth hummus is not too sweet. It makes enough for a party, but you could eat enough to unintentionally make it a meal.

//

Drain and rinse the garbanzo beans and place them in a food processor. Add the stock and lemon juice.

Add the onion, garlic, cilantro, and parsley to the food processor along with the curry powder. Blend until smooth, about 3 minutes. Add salt and pepper to taste. Blend for 15 seconds. Taste and adjust if necessary. Blend for another minute. Serve in a bowl with carrot sticks—they'll pick up the sweetness from The Roots Stock and it's tremendous.

Caramelized Onion Bread Pudding

Serves 4

2 tablespoons butter, divided

1 loaf Italian white bread

1 teaspoon olive oil

1 small yellow onion

Pinch of kosher salt and black pepper

1 cup The Roots Stock (page xviii)

¼ cup heavy cream

½ teaspoon dried thyme

⅓ cup (1 ounce) blue cheese crumbles, plus more for garnish

This side dish is a supporting actor that ends up stealing the show. The butter, cheese, and heavy cream take the place of more traditional egg and lend a richness to balance out the luscious onions and The Roots Stock. Sweet and savory in each bite, this one will make you forget about your steak for a while.

///

Preheat the oven to 200°F. Grease 4 ramekins (3½ to 4½ inches in diameter) or an 8 by 8-inch glass baking dish with butter. Set aside.

Cut the bread into 1-inch-thick slices and then cube. You should end up with about 4 cups (you'll use about half a regular loaf). Place a single layer of the bread cubes on a baking sheet and barely drizzle olive oil on top. Bake for 20 minutes or longer, until the bread is dry and feels slightly stiff. Remove from the oven, set the bread aside in a large bowl, and raise the oven temperature to 400°F.

Peel off the skin and slice your onion into ⅛-inch-thick slices. Melt 1 tablespoon of butter in a large saucepan over medium heat. Add the onion and stir every few minutes. If the onions turn black, add a spoonful of water and turn the heat down slightly.

After 30 minutes, when the onions have started to caramelize, add a pinch of salt and pepper along with the stock, cream, and thyme. Stir gently with a wooden spoon, scraping up any onion bits stuck to the pan. Raise the heat to high and bring to a boil. Once boiling, remove from the heat and pour the liquid and onions over the bread in the bowl.

Stir gently to coat the bread evenly. It should soak up most of the liquid. Mix in the ⅓ cup blue cheese gently to avoid smashing the bread. Place the bread in the ramekins or the prepared baking dish.

If you're baking the bread in the ramekins, bake for 15 to 20 minutes, until golden brown. If you're using the baking dish, bake for 25 to 30 minutes. You can add a few crumbles of blue cheese to the top for garnish before serving.

Gentle Pig Stock

Alex Pope, Kansas City, Missouri

Makes 2 to 2½ quarts

2 pounds pork neck or leg bones

3 quarts (12 cups) cold water

4 medium shallots

1 head garlic

**1 tablespoon plus 1 teaspoon
whole black peppercorns**

2 tablespoons mustard seeds

3 tablespoons apple cider vinegar

1 tablespoon kosher salt

This stock proves that pork can be light if freed from the heavy influence of smoke. The Gentle Pig Stock pours a beautiful chestnut brown that will settle to a lighter shade overnight. And while pork provides a subtle backbone, the shallots shine through in a fashion that evokes French onion soup. This stock is easy to execute and is malleable enough to work into soups and dishes, and as braising liquid.

//

Rinse the bones in cold water if you see bone dust, a fine white powder created when the bones are cut with a saw. Pat dry with a paper towel. Place the bones in an 8-quart stockpot and add the water.

Slice the shallots into medium-thin coin-shaped slices, about the thickness of a quarter. Cut the garlic head in half horizontally. Add the shallot slices and garlic halves, including the skin, to the pot. Next add the peppercorns, mustard seeds, vinegar, and salt.

Turn the heat to medium-high. Once bubbles break the surface, about 20 minutes, turn the heat down to medium-low. Keep the stock at a steady simmer for 4 hours total. Don't worry about skimming; you'll be straining later. You're shooting for about a bubble per second and no more than 4 bubbles per second.

Remove the stockpot from the heat. Place a large metal bowl or pot beneath a fine-mesh strainer or colander and ladle in the stock. You're going to strain the stock again. Line the strainer with a slightly damp coffee filter (#6) and add the stock. After the second pass, fill your sink with cold water and ice and submerge the metal container with stock in the ice bath. Stir the stock every 15 minutes to help release heat. At the same time, you can drain some water and add more ice.

Once your food is 40°F, it's safe to place the bowl or pot of stock in your fridge. Store in an airtight container for 2 to 4 days. If you want to freeze the stock, pour it into a freezer-safe container with the lid off. Leave ½ inch to 1 inch of space to allow for the stock to expand. After 6 hours in the freezer, place the lid on your stock and label it with the date it's frozen. You'll want to use it within 4 months.

TO ENJOY AS A DRINKING BROTH: Pour 1 cup of hot stock into a mug or French press. Add a sprig of oregano and steep for 10 minutes. Remove the oregano. Salt to taste. If you want it spicy, you can add a few drops of chili oil and 1 finely chopped green onion. You could also doctor it up with ground ginger, finely chopped scallions, mustard seeds, garlic powder, and nori (seaweed).

Posole Verde

Todd Schulte, Uncommon Stock, Kansas City, Missouri

Serves 6 to 8

2 poblano chiles

Olive oil

1 tablespoon cumin seeds

½ teaspoon anise seeds

1 large white onion

3 tablespoons canola oil
(or vegetable oil)

1½ tablespoons chopped garlic, divided

9 cups Gentle Pig Stock (page 6)

1¼ pounds boneless, skinless chicken
breasts (or 5 chicken breast halves)

4 medium Yukon Gold potatoes

3 (15-ounce) cans white hominy

1 jalapeño

5 chiles de árbol

¾ pound tomatillos

½ bunch fresh cilantro leaves,
chopped, plus more for garnish

4 leaves romaine lettuce

½ tablespoon Mexican dried oregano

Kosher salt and freshly ground
black pepper

Radishes, sliced (optional)

Avocado, sliced (optional)

Queso fresco, crumbled (optional)

Toasty. Spicy. Sweet. Posole Verde is a Mexican soup/stew with gorgeous layers of flavor that are worth all of the steps in this recipe. The Gentle Pig Stock marries well with the hominy and offers a subtle twist.

//

Preheat the oven to 400°F. Rub the poblano chiles with olive oil and roast for 15 minutes, until the skins start to blister. Remove the chiles from the oven and set aside on a plate to cool.

Heat a small skillet or frying pan over high heat. Place the cumin seeds in the pan when it's hot. Hold the pan's handle and roll your wrist to shake the seeds and keep them from sticking. Let the seeds toast for about 1 minute, until they darken slightly and you can smell them. Remove the seeds from the heat and set aside on a plate to cool.

(continued)

Posole Verde (continued)

Place the cooled seeds in a plastic bag and crush them with a rolling pin or the bottom of a pan. Repeat the process with the anise seeds, though they may need 2 to 3 minutes of toasting. Combine the spices in a small bowl and set aside.

Peel and roughly chop the onion. Place the canola oil in a heavy-bottomed stockpot on medium-high heat. Add the onions and 1 tablespoon of the garlic to the pan and cook until the onions are translucent, 8 to 10 minutes. Add the cumin and anise and stir gently to coat the onions and garlic with the spices. Then add the stock and chicken.

Simmer the chicken in the stock until it's cooked through (the internal temperature should be at least 165°F). The meat will no longer be pink, and the juices will be clear. Remove the chicken from the pot and let it cool on a cutting board. When it's cool enough to handle, shred it with your hands.

Rinse, peel, and dice the potatoes into ¼-inch cubes. Rinse and drain the hominy. Add the potatoes and hominy to the pot and simmer until the potatoes are tender, 20 to 25 minutes.

Stem, skin, and seed the roasted poblano chiles. Cut off the tip of the jalapeño and stand the chile upright with the stem up. Slice from the top, curving the blade slightly in as you chop down. Rotate the jalapeño and keep slicing. Discard the stem and seeds, and remove any seeds stuck to the flesh. Cut it into strips. Roll the chiles de árbol between your fingers to loosen the seeds inside. Break the chiles in half with your fingers and shake the seeds loose. Discard the seeds. Place all of the peppers in a blender.

Husk and quarter the tomatillos, and rinse and chop the cilantro and romaine lettuce. Add the tomatillos, cilantro, and romaine to the blender, along with the remaining ½ tablespoon garlic, oregano, and a pinch of salt and black pepper. Blend on high, 3 to 4 minutes, until the ingredients are well combined.

When the potatoes are tender, add the contents of the blender and the shredded chicken back into the soup. Let it simmer for 5 minutes, then taste the soup and add salt and pepper if needed. Ladle the posole into bowls and garnish with sliced radishes, avocado, and queso fresco.

Red Beans & Rice

Serves 6

1 pound dried red kidney beans

½ pound andouille sausage

2 tablespoons Gentle Pig Stock fat
(bacon grease or butter)

1 medium yellow onion

1 celery stalk

1 green bell pepper

2 cloves garlic, minced

8 cups (2 quarts) Gentle Pig Stock
(page 6)

1 pound smoked ham hock
(or smoked turkey leg)

2 bay leaves

Pinch of cayenne pepper

1 teaspoon dried thyme

Kosher salt and freshly ground
black pepper

2 cups long-grain white rice

1 tablespoon butter (or schmaltz)

Tabasco sauce, for garnish

2 or 3 green onions, chopped, for garnish

Whether you're doing hard work or avoiding it, there's comfort to be found in red beans and rice. The sausage and ham hock lend a smoky flair to the beans that are imbued with the goodness of pork. This version doesn't stray far from a classic Southern preparation, and it lets you use a little bit of the fat that you've got on hand from making stock.

//

Place the dried beans in a medium stockpot and cover completely with room-temperature water. Soak overnight. Drain and then rinse the beans one more time before you begin cooking. If you weren't able to plan ahead, you can quick-soak the beans by bringing 10 cups of water to a boil in a medium saucepan. Rinse and drain the dried beans, add to the saucepan, and let the water come to a boil again. Cook for 1 minute and then remove from the heat. Cover the pan, and let it sit for 1 hour to 90 minutes.

(continued)

Red Beans & Rice (continued)

Slice the andouille sausage into ½-inch-thick rounds on the diagonal. Add the stock fat to a Dutch oven or heavy-bottomed stockpot over medium-high heat. Cook the sausage until browned, 3 to 5 minutes per side.

While the sausage is browning, peel and dice the onion into ¼-inch chunks. Cut the celery stalk to the same size. Remove the stem and seeds from the green bell pepper and chop as fine as the onions and celery. You want a pile of onions equal to the pile of celery and peppers.

Remove the sausage from the heat and set aside on a plate.

Add the onions, celery, green bell pepper, and garlic to the pot. Stir occasionally until the onions turn translucent, 7 to 10 minutes. Add the stock, beans, ham hock, bay leaves, cayenne pepper, and thyme. Turn the heat to high and bring the pot to a boil.

Decrease the heat to low and once you see the surface gently simmering, cover the pot and cook for 2 hours. After 1 hour, add the sausage to the pot and scrape a wooden spoon along the bottom of the pan to make sure the beans aren't sticking. Remove the ham hock at the same time and chop it into fine pieces. Add the pieces back into the pot. If the beans are not completely covered, add ¼ to ½ cup of stock.

Cover the beans again. At 2 hours, check to see if the beans are creamy. If they are, take a page from chef Emeril Lagasse and mash one-quarter of the beans against the side of the pot with a wooden spoon. (This will add some different textures to the rice and beans. It's well worth it.) Remove the bay leaves. Season to taste with salt and pepper.

To cook the rice—which you'll want to do roughly 30 minutes before you serve the rice and beans—place it in a metal strainer. Rinse the rice two or three times under cold water, tamping it down and stirring it a bit while the water is flowing. Drain off the excess water and place the rice in a medium saucepan.

Add 3 cups of water (or Gentle Pig Stock) to the saucepan along with the butter and 1 teaspoon salt. Turn the heat to medium-high and bring the rice to a boil. Once it's boiling, turn the heat to medium-low. Place the cover on the pan and simmer for 15 minutes.

Remove the pan from the heat and let the rice rest for another 5 minutes. Fluff the rice with a fork.

Place a heaping scoop of rice in a flat-bottomed dish or bowl and then ladle the beans over it. Garnish with a splash of Tabasco and chopped green onion.

Chileatole

Patrick Ryan, Port Fonda, Kansas City, Missouri

Serves 6 to 8

PORK & CORN STOCK

4 pounds pork bones

4 ears corn

Cold water, for simmering

2 tablespoons olive oil

½ large white onion

1 serrano chile

5 cloves garlic

4 ears corn

**2 chiles de árbol
(3 if very small or if you like it spicy)**

5 quarts (20 cups) Pork & Corn Stock

**4 epazote leaves (or 1 teaspoon
dried epazote), see Note**

Kosher salt and white sugar

Think of this as a slightly spicy cousin to corn chowder, wherein the corn provides the creaminess without the need for any cream. This savory Mexican soup gets earthiness from the chiles and pork stock and has just the right lightness for summer.

//

To make the stock, preheat the oven to 375°F. Roast the pork bones on a baking sheet for 15 minutes or until they turn brown and give off a roasted smell. Shuck and cut the ears of corn in half. Place in a large stockpot.

Add the pork bones to the stockpot and enough water to cover the bones and corncobs. Turn the heat to high and bring the water to a simmer. When bubbles begin breaking the surface, turn the heat down to low and simmer for 4 hours. Remove the pot from the heat and strain the stock. Discard the solids. Refrigerate in an airtight container for up to 3 days.

To make the Chileatole, place the olive oil in the bottom of a large stockpot over medium heat. Peel the onion, chop off the root, and dice it into large pieces, about 6 cuts lengthwise and widthwise. Remove the stem from the serrano chile, and halve, peel, and smash the garlic cloves. Add the onion, serrano chile, and garlic cloves to the pot.

Cook for 3 to 5 minutes, until the onion turns translucent—you don't want it to brown. Shuck the corn and scrape off the kernels. Add the kernels, cob, and chiles de árbol to the pot. Continue cooking over medium heat until the kernels change from pale yellow to bright yellow in color, about 3 minutes.

Add the Pork & Corn Stock and turn the heat to high. Bring the stock to a simmer and adjust the heat down to medium to keep it at a simmer for 15 minutes. Remove the pot from the heat and take out the corncobs. Add the epazote leaves. Use a handheld blender to blend into a drinkable broth, the consistency of heated cream.

Strain the soup through a fine-mesh strainer. Add salt and sugar to taste. Serve hot in bowls.

NOTE: Epazote is sold everywhere from Mexican markets to Walmart. If either has epazote in stock, you're also likely to find chiles de árbol and serrano chiles a little farther down the aisle.

Beef Stock

Alex Pope, Kansas City, Missouri

Makes 2 to 2½ quarts

2 tablespoons dried porcini mushrooms

1 pound beef marrow bones

5 pounds beef knuckle bones
(neck bones or meaty bones)

3 quarts (12 cups) water

¼ cup red wine vinegar

2 tablespoons kosher salt

1 large red onion

2 heads garlic

12 sprigs (¾ ounce) fresh oregano

5 or 6 sprigs (¾ ounce)
fresh rosemary

5 tablespoons coriander

2 bay leaves

A sheep farmer once told me that great sheep's-milk cheese has some sheep to it—a little bit of the grass and world that the fluffy four-leggers inhabit. This stock invokes that same principle. It's got some earthiness and an almost grassy character, from the herbs and toasted mushrooms (which will call to mind Marsala while they're cooking), before you get to the big, deep beef body that will speak to carnivores.

//

Preheat the oven to 300°F. Spread the dried mushrooms in a single layer on a baking sheet. Toast for 6 to 8 minutes, until you can smell a toasty earthiness from the mushrooms in the oven. Remove the sheet and place the mushrooms on a plate or in a bowl. Set aside.

Place the marrow bones and beef knuckle bones in a large stockpot (at least 8 quarts). Add the water, vinegar, and salt.

Remove the skin from the red onion and cut it into thick slices, roughly the thickness of half your pinkie. Add the onion slices to the pot with the whole garlic heads and dried mushrooms.

Rinse and pat dry the oregano and rosemary. Add to the pot with the coriander and bay leaves. Turn the heat to medium-high. Once bubbles break the surface, about 20 minutes, turn the heat down to medium-low. You never want the stock to reach a rolling boil; instead keep it at a steady simmer for 5 hours. You're shooting for about a bubble per second and no more than 4 bubbles per second.

Remove the stockpot from the heat. Place a large metal bowl or pot beneath a fine-mesh strainer or colander and ladle in the stock. You're going to strain the stock again. Line the strainer with a slightly damp coffee filter (#6) and add the stock. After the second pass, fill your sink with cold water and ice and submerge the metal container with stock in the ice bath. Stir the stock every 15 minutes to help release heat. At the same time, you can drain some water and add more ice. Once your food is 40°F, it's safe to place the bowl or pot of stock in your fridge. Store in an airtight container for 2 to 4 days. If you want to freeze the stock, pour it into a freezer-safe container with the lid off. Leave ½ inch to 1 inch of space to allow for the stock to expand. After 6 hours in the freezer, place the lid on your stock and label it with the date it's frozen. You'll want to use it within 4 months.

TO ENJOY AS A DRINKING BROTH: Pour 1 cup of hot stock into a mug or French press. Add a sprig of rosemary and thyme and steep for 10 minutes. Remove the herbs. Salt to taste. For an even richer version, you can add some of the marrow from the bones in the stock and a bit of balsamic vinegar to balance it out. You could also walk out the door with the beginnings of soup courtesy of black peppercorns and a fine dice of carrots, celery, and green onion.

NOTE: Fresh herbs are typically sold in the grocery store in .75- or .8-ounce containers. If you're shopping at a market or from your garden, just grab a bundle of sprigs.

Stockyard Bison Chili

Serves 6 to 8

2 tablespoons olive oil, divided

1 pound ground bison

1 tablespoon kosher salt, divided

1 tablespoon black pepper, divided

1 cup Beef Stock (page 16), divided

1 large yellow onion, diced

4 cloves garlic, minced

2 (14.5-ounce) cans diced tomatoes

1 (14.5-ounce) can pinto beans

1 (14.5-ounce) can dark red kidney beans

1 (14.5-ounce) can light red kidney beans

¼ teaspoon paprika

¼ teaspoon turmeric

¼ teaspoon cumin

¼ teaspoon chili powder

⅓ teaspoon nutmeg

½ teaspoon cinnamon

Pinch of garlic powder

12 whole coriander seeds

¾ cup (6 ounces) Pilsner

Hot sauce (optional)

Shredded cheddar cheese, for garnish

Chili is for football Sundays and the victors of snowball fights. This robust bowl is worthy of weekend champions. The lean bison cooked in the beefy stock gives the chili a roundness without making it too heavy. This is a balanced bowl with a lot of spices, but you'll end up tweaking it based on your mood and who will be joining you at the dinner table. Make this a day ahead and let your fridge do a little flavor alchemy.

//

Place 1 tablespoon of olive oil in a cast iron pan (or skillet) and turn the heat to medium-high. Generously season the ground bison with salt and pepper. When the oil is shimmering, but not smoking, add the bison. Sear on each side for about 5 minutes, until a brown crust forms. Add ½ cup of Beef Stock to the pan and cook for an additional 10 minutes.

While the bison is cooking, heat the remaining 1 tablespoon of oil in a Dutch oven or 6-quart stockpot on medium high heat. Add the onion and garlic and stir every few minutes with a wooden spoon. When the onion turns translucent, add 1 can of diced tomatoes and the remaining ½ cup Beef Stock.

In a colander, drain and rinse the pinto, dark red kidney, and light red kidney beans. Add them to the pot along with the paprika, turmeric, cumin, chili powder, nutmeg, cinnamon, and garlic powder. Use the flat side of a knife to crack the coriander seeds before adding them to the pot.

Next, add the bison and drippings from the skillet and the second can of tomatoes. Pour in the beer. Stir the pot to mix together the ingredients. Let the chili come to a boil and then turn the heat down to medium so the top is an active simmer (bubbles consistently breaking the surface). Now, wait the time it takes you to drink the remaining half of the Pilsner, about 30 minutes.

Taste the chili. The flavors won't be completely blended, but you're just looking to see if it has gone too far in any one direction (sweet or salty). Add salt or pepper or a bit more cinnamon or a splash of hot sauce. Remember, you're not trying to finish it here, just work on the balance.

Let it simmer for at least 3 hours on the stove. The surface of the chili can be active, you just don't want to see a lot of steam leaving the pot. Remove the pot from the heat and place in an ice bath. Once the chili's temperature is 40°F, place in the refrigerator overnight.

The next day, you can heat the chili on the stovetop or in individual bowls in the microwave. Taste and season with salt or pepper, and garnish with shredded cheddar cheese or a splash of hot sauce. If you have leftovers, they'll keep in an airtight container in the fridge for another 2 to 3 days.

Chuck Eye Pot Roast

Serves 6 to 8

3 tablespoons olive oil, divided

3½ pounds chuck eye roast

Kosher salt and freshly ground
black pepper

2 large yellow onions

4 cloves garlic

6 large carrots

1 cup red wine

3 cups Beef Stock (page 16)

1 pound baby potatoes

2 sprigs fresh thyme

2 bay leaves

Crusty bread, for serving

This is a conversation stopper. It arrives on the table and the aroma of the rich gravy will have your guests breathing deeply as if they were in a lozenge commercial. After that, it's all forks hitting the bottoms of the plates and requests for more pot roast. The carrots and potatoes have just enough give to soak up some of the gravy but still provide a bit of textural balance to the tender beef.

//

Preheat the oven to 275°F. In a Dutch oven over medium-high heat, heat 2 tablespoons of the olive oil. Pat dry the chuck eye roast with a paper towel, and then season with salt and pepper. Place the roast in the pot and let it brown for a little over 1 minute on each side—you want a good sear. Remove to a plate and set aside.

Add the remaining 1 tablespoon of olive oil to the pot. Decrease the heat to medium. Peel and quarter the onions and peel the skin off the garlic cloves. Sweat the garlic and onions for 4 minutes, flipping halfway through, until they're slightly caramelized. Remove them from the pot and place in a large bowl. Set aside.

(continued)

21

Chuck Eye Pot Roast (continued)

Peel the carrots and chop into 2-inch pieces. Place them in the pot with the oil for a minute or two, turning them with a spatula or wooden spoon until they just start to brown. Add the carrots to the bowl with the onions and garlic. Set aside.

Add the red wine to the pot and, while the steam rises, deglaze the bottom, scraping off the stuck browned bits of meat and vegetables. Return the roast to the pot and pour in the Beef Stock. The liquid should be between halfway and three-fourths of the way up the sides of the roast. Use a baster or spoon to add liquid to the top of the meat.

Add the onions, carrots, and garlic to the pot. Rinse and halve the potatoes. Then layer the potatoes atop the roast and vegetables and the thyme and bay leaves on top of the potatoes. Cover the pot and place it in the oven to cook for approximately 4 hours.

After 3½ hours, check the roast with a fork. If it separates with no effort, you're done. If not, keep it in the oven and repeat the fork test every 15 or 20 minutes. Remove the bay leaves. Serve in a bowl or deep plate with crusty bread on the side—you'll want something to sop up the sauce. The pot roast will keep in an airtight container in the fridge for 2 days.

Carnivore Stock

Alex Pope, Kansas City, Missouri

Makes 2 to 2½ quarts

1 tablespoon extra-virgin olive oil

1 large yellow onion

1 pound bacon

1 head garlic

4 large sprigs (¾ ounce) fresh sage

12 sprigs (¾ ounce) fresh thyme

2 tablespoons dry white wine

2 pounds chicken bones

3½ pounds beef knuckle bones (or neck bones)

3 pounds pork leg or neck bones

3 quarts (12 cups) cold water

½ cup apple cider vinegar

This is like the liquids from braised meats got together to throw a party in your stockpot. It's smoky from the bacon and sweet from the onions, with a little bit of the peat that one gets from good Scotch—the flavor wheel is spinning at the stock carnival. It's akin to a meatball because of the three different meats that provide the luscious base, which is simultaneously complex and familiar.

//

Place the olive oil in a skillet (cast iron if you have it on hand). Heat the pan on medium-high heat until the oil is shimmering. Snip off the tip and root from the onion, cut it in half horizontally, and remove the skin. Cut the onion from root to stem into slices a little thinner than a pencil. Add the slices to the pan and gently toss them in the oil.

While the onions are cooking, roughly chop the bacon into ½-inch squares. Set aside. Slice the head of garlic in half lengthwise. Rinse and pat dry the sage and thyme. Set them aside.

As the onions cook, turn down the heat if you see them developing dark brown or black spots. Check the onions every 6 to 8 minutes, scraping up the fond (the sugar released from the onions that forms a glaze on the bottom of the skillet).

If the onions stick too much, add a tablespoon of broth or paper-thin slice of butter. After about 40 minutes on the stove, the onions should be golden in color and have the sweetness you want. The longer you keep them on, the darker and richer the caramel color and flavor.

Remove the onions from the skillet and place them in a small bowl. Add the wine to the skillet. As the liquid bubbles, scrape up the browned bits with a spatula or wooden spoon. Add those bits to the bowl with the onions. Set aside.

Place the chicken, beef, and pork bones in a large stockpot. Add the water and vinegar. Then layer in the onions, bacon, garlic, sage, and thyme. Turn the heat to medium-high.

Once bubbles break the surface, about 20 minutes, turn the heat down to medium-low. You never want the stock to reach a rolling boil; instead keep it at a steady simmer for 5 hours. You're shooting for about a bubble per second and no more than 4 bubbles per second. You don't need to skim because you'll be straining.

Remove the stockpot from the heat. Place a large metal bowl or pot beneath a fine-mesh strainer or colander and ladle in the stock. You're going to strain the stock again. Line the strainer with a slightly damp coffee filter (#6) and add the stock. After the second pass, fill your sink with cold water and ice and submerge the metal container with stock in the ice bath. Stir the stock every 15 minutes to help release heat. At the same time, you can drain some water and add more ice. Once your food is 40°F, it's safe to place the bowl or pot of stock in your fridge. Store in an airtight container for 2 to 4 days. If you want to freeze the stock, pour it into a freezer-safe container with the lid off. Leave ½ inch to 1 inch of space to allow for the stock to expand. After 6 hours in the freezer, place the lid on your stock and label it with the date it's frozen. You'll want to use it within 4 months.

TO ENJOY AS A DRINKING BROTH: Pour 1 cup of hot stock into a mug or French press. Add a few sprigs of parsley and steep for 10 minutes. Remove the herbs. Salt to taste. You could also steep a few 1-inch coins of fresh ginger and star anise seeds, or try a blend of tarragon, chives, and whole black peppercorns.

French Onion Soup

Serves 6

3 pounds yellow onions
(6 medium onions)

4 tablespoons (½ stick)
unsalted butter

2 cloves garlic, minced

Kosher salt and freshly ground
black pepper

8 cups (2 quarts) Carnivore Stock
(page 24)

½ cup sherry (or dry white wine)

1 bay leaf

2 sprigs fresh thyme

1 pound Gruyère cheese

1 baguette

Extra-virgin olive oil, for brushing

Axl Rose sang all we need is just a little patience. And, oh, must he have been singing about this soup. Everything—in particular, the glorious smell of onions caramelizing—will tell you to rush and get this soup in a bowl as quickly as you can. But if you are a bit intentional about the timing—crusty bread and bubbly cheese are a must—the wait is well worth it.

//

Peel the onions. Cut off the root and then slice them into ⅛-inch-thick half-moons; slice those moons down the middle. You should end up with 6 to 8 cups. Melt the butter in a wide, heavy-bottomed saucepan over medium-high heat. Once the butter foams, add the onions and garlic along with a pinch of salt and pepper. Stir the onions to coat them evenly in butter and turn the heat down to medium.

Let the onions caramelize over a period of at least 30 minutes, stirring every few minutes; don't let them blacken. Turn down the heat slightly or add a bit of water or butter if they're starting to stick too much or get too dark. Black onions will make your soup bitter.

After the onions have been cooking for 15 minutes, add the stock to a separate pot and warm it on medium-low heat. Once the onions have caramelized, add the sherry and bring it to a boil. Scrape any browned bits off the bottom of the pan. Lower the heat to a simmer and cook for about 4 minutes, until you can't smell the alcohol in the sherry. Add the bay leaf, thyme, and warm stock to the pot. Bring the soup to a slow simmer—a few bubbles, not froth on the surface. Partially cover the pan and let it simmer for at least 30 minutes.

Grate the Gruyère into a bowl and set aside. You're going to want to start this last step 15 to 20 minutes before you're ready to serve the soup.

Move a rack to the top position in the oven. Set the broiler to low and preheat the oven for about 10 minutes. Cut the baguette into 1-inch-thick slices and brush them lightly with olive oil. You will need 1½ times as many slices as people you're serving (i.e., 9 slices for 6 people). Place them on a baking sheet and into the oven. Broil for 2 minutes, or until golden brown, and remove the baking tray from the oven. Use tongs to flip the bread on the baking sheet.

Generously cover the bread slices with three-fourths of the grated cheese. Put back in the oven for 1 to 3 minutes. Keep a close eye on the bread—you want the cheese brown and bubbly, not burned.

Remove the sheet from the oven and use tongs to transfer the bread in a single layer to a plate or cutting board. You'll want a half-slice for the bottom of each soup bowl and a full slice for the top. Place a half-slice in each soup bowl. Add a small sprinkle of Gruyère. Ladle in the soup to about ½ inch below the rim of the bowl. Add a generous sprinkle of Gruyère on top of the soup, along with a full slice of bread.

Ancho Chile Chicken Tacos & Guacamole

Serves 4 to 6

ANCHO CHILE CHICKEN

1½ tablespoons olive oil

6 chicken thighs

1 medium yellow onion, diced

1 red bell pepper, seeded and diced

1 celery stalk, diced

4 cloves garlic, minced

1½ teaspoons smoked paprika

1 teaspoon paprika

1 teaspoon cumin

2 teaspoons ancho chile powder

Pinch of nutmeg

Kosher salt and freshly ground black pepper

Red wine (or beer)

3 cups Carnivore Stock (page 24)

GUACAMOLE

2 avocados

¼ cup minced red onion, plus more for garnish

3 tablespoons finely chopped fresh cilantro, plus more for garnish

1 tablespoon freshly squeezed lemon juice

1 tablespoon freshly squeezed lime juice

½ small tomato

½ teaspoon kosher salt

Freshly ground black pepper

Taco night doesn't mean you have to settle. Tender chicken sits in this rich, deep red sauce that is subtly smoky, redolent, and addictive. The guacamole adds brightness with the citrus and red onion in addition to lovely color. This dish makes plenty of sauce if you want to serve it over rice—and don't forget the tortillas.

///

(continued)

Ancho Chile Chicken Tacos & Guacamole (continued)

To make your taco filling, place the olive oil in a Dutch oven and heat on medium-high. Rinse the chicken thighs and pat them dry with a paper towel. Place them skin side down in the pot and cook for 3 to 5 minutes on 1 side, until browned. Remove the chicken and set aside on a plate.

After you remove the chicken, add the onion, pepper, celery, garlic, smoked paprika, paprika, cumin, ancho chile powder, nutmeg, salt, and pepper to the pot. Lower the heat to medium. Stir together and cook for 3 to 5 minutes, until the onions start to feel soft. Next, add a splash of red wine to scrape up any browned bits on the bottom of the pan.

Return the chicken to the pot. Add the stock. You want the liquid to be between one-half and three-fourths of the way up the sides of the chicken. Bring the stock to a steady simmer, where a few bubbles are breaking the surface, but it's not frothy. Cover and check after 1 hour. If the meat separates from the bone, the chicken is done. If not, let it cook another 20 minutes and try again. Once the chicken is cooked, carefully remove it from the pan to a cutting board. Let it cool for a minute, then shred it with a pair of forks. Pull out the fat and bones and set aside. Return the shredded chicken to the braising liquid.

You can store the chicken and sauce overnight— the flavors will meld nicely— or serve it hot. If you are serving it the next day, you can skim off the fat and bring up the heat slowly to warm. Leftovers will keep in an airtight container in the refrigerator for 2 to 3 days.

To make the guacamole, cut the avocados in half, remove the pits, and spoon the flesh into a medium bowl. Add the onion and cilantro to the avocado.

Add the lemon and lime juice to the bowl. (Cut a few lime slices for the tacos as well.) Remove the seeds and pulp from the tomato (you can use the other half as a taco topping) and roughly chop the flesh. Add the tomatoes to the bowl and mix together with a fork. Use enough force to break up the avocado, but don't beat it up. After the onions and tomato are spread throughout the bowl, add the salt and pepper to taste. Taste again and adjust the citrus, cilantro, or salt to your liking. Serve immediately.

Broth Cocktails

Sometimes the only thing separating a mixologist and a chef is where their respective pig tattoos happen to be located. Both are taking cues from each other, leading to a new wave of savory cocktails that use broth as a flavoring agent or base. Umami is now as exciting a flavor as sweet, and a slow cooker is not an uncommon sight behind a trendy bar as the temperature dips.

Although you may have seen a strip of bacon sticking out of an ornately decorated Bloody Mary, there are other, more subtle ways that carnivores have been attempting to sneak meat into cocktails. Fat-washing, essentially infusing spirits with the taste of a given fat (it could range from bacon to truffle oil), has recently become a trendy technique to add meatiness to a cocktail without the associated greasiness. The infused spirit is chilled in the freezer so a bartender can skim off the fat, which goes from a liquid to a solid but leaves behind the essence.

Still, imbuing a bit of meaty goodness via stock is not a new addition to cocktails. There's a classic drink—the Bloody Bull—a cousin to the Bloody Mary, which adds beef stock or bouillon to the equation. The Bull Shot, which directly swaps in beef stock for tomato juice, is its (wisely) less popular relative.

In the following pages, mixologist Arturo Vera-Felicie, of the Justus Drugstore in Smithville, Missouri, offers his version of the Bloody Bull along with a trio of stock cocktails designed to be served warm. If you're making multiple cocktails, you can keep the stock warm in a slow cooker set on low to avoid over-reducing. And for those who are vegetarian or vegan, the warm drinks include a root vegetable cocktail.

Bloody Bull

Arturo Vera-Felicie, Justus Drugstore, Smithville, Missouri

Serves 1

COCKTAIL

2 dashes celery bitters

4 dashes Tabasco sauce

1 dash freshly squeezed orange juice

Pinch of black pepper

1 teaspoon whole-grain mustard

2 ounces Beef Stock (page 16)

2 ounces vodka

2 ounces Sacramento tomato juice

Ice

GARNISH

Orange peel

Whole cloves

A bit more body and a lot more interesting than your standard Bloody Mary, this Bloody Bull kick-starts brunch. Vera-Felicie's honors renowned mixologist Dale DeGroff's contention that savory elements can work in a cocktail. Here, celery bitters take the place of the standard celery stalk, while the zing of mustard creates what Vera-Felicie refers to simply as s"the jam."

///

Place the celery bitters, Tabasco, orange juice, black pepper, mustard, stock, vodka, and tomato juice in a mixing glass. Shake until your ingredients are well combined. Fill a goblet with ice and pour in the cocktail.

For the garnish, use a vegetable peeler to create a 1-inch-wide by 3-inch-long slice of orange peel (or as close as you can get). Push the pointy end of a clove into the peel, just until it sticks in the skin, about every ¼ inch or so. Hang the peel over the rim of your glass.

"With mustard and beef and mustard and tomato, you've got a flavor bridge right there. You take two ingredients that are so far apart, and they each have something in common with that third ingredient. Here, mustard is that flavor bridge," says Arturo Vera-Felicie.

Pig Man on Campus (PMOC)

Arturo Vera-Felicie, Justus Drugstore, Smithville, Missouri

Serves 1

COCKTAIL

4½ ounces Gentle Pig Stock (page 6)

1½ ounces amontillado sherry (or medium-dry sherry)

1 bar spoon (about ⅛ ounce) Pedro Ximénez sherry

3 dashes Angostura bitters

GARNISH

1 onion slice

1 celery slice

1 carrot stick

This is a fireplace cocktail inspired by the traditional use of sherry and Angostura bitters as flavoring in soups. There should be snow on the ground, so the drink, which pinballs between sweet—the sherry lends some raisin notes—and savory and salty, can give you that warm, gooey feeling inside.

//

Bring the stock to a boil over medium-high heat. After that, turn the heat down to medium or medium-low to keep a gentle simmer. Cover the pot with a lid so you don't over-reduce. You want your stock to be hot but not boiling, as if you were steeping tea.

You'll also want to warm the glass or mug you'll be using to serve the cocktail by filling it with hot water until the glass or mug feels warm to the touch. This will help keep the cocktail warm and open up the aromatics you add to the drink.

Place the warm stock in your warmed mug. Add the sherries and Angostura bitters. Mix gently with a bar spoon until well combined.

For the garnish, you can create a mirepoix skewer by sticking an onion slice and celery slice on either end of a carrot stick, using the carrot stick as your skewer. You can then rest the stick on the top of the glass or serve alongside your cocktail.

Gin & Jus

Serves 1

4 ½ ounces Carnivore Stock (page 24)

1½ ounces genever
(Boomsma Oude, see Note)

3 dashes orange bitters
(Regan's Orange Bitters No. 6)

5 drops orange blossom water

3 drops saline

Sprig of sage or thyme, for garnish

This one is for the meat-lovers. The drink starts with an oakiness—Boomsma Oude is aged in oak barrels for about a year—that leads to a rich, meaty center. The two play off each other like whiskey and bacon. The orange blossom water adds a touch of sweetness at the end that lightens up the full-bodied cocktail.

///

Bring the stock to a boil over medium-high heat, then turn the heat down to medium or medium-low to keep a gentle simmer. Cover the pot with a lid so you don't over-reduce it. You want your stock to be hot, but not boiling, as if you were steeping tea.

You'll also want to warm the glass or mug you'll be using to serve the cocktail by putting hot water inside it until the glass or mug feels warm to the touch. This will help keep the cocktail warm and open up the aromatics you add to the drink.

Place the warm stock in the warmed mug. Add the genever, orange bitters, and orange blossom water. Mix three parts salt to seven parts water to make the saline. Add three drops to the warmed glass or mug. Discard or store the extra saline in a dropper bottle. Garnish with a sprig of sage or thyme.

Note: Before there was dry gin in England, there was genever made from malted grains in Holland. If you can't find Boomsma or genever, look for a lemony, dry gin like Beefeater—a gin that has been rested in barrels.

Root Seller

Arturo Vera-Felicie, Justus Drugstore, Smithville, Missouri

Serves 1

4½ ounces The Roots Stock (page xviii)

5 drops saline

1½ ounces aquavit (akvavit)

3 dashes celery bitters

Carrot top, for garnish

This winter warmer will make you long for spring. It's light and bright and emphasizes the fennel in the stock, but it also has these lovely bits of caraway and anise from the aquavit. It's a cocktail that will make you rethink what you can do with stock.

//

Bring the stock to a boil over medium-high heat. After that, turn the heat down to medium or medium-low to keep it at a gentle simmer. Cover the pot with a lid so you don't over-reduce. You want your stock to be hot but not boiling, as if you were steeping tea.

You'll also want to warm the glass or mug you'll be using to serve the cocktail by filling it with hot water until the glass or mug feels warm to the touch.

Mix 3 parts salt to 7 parts water to make the saline. Add 5 drops to the warmed mug or glass. Pour in the stock, aquavit, and celery bitters. Stir gently with a bar spoon until well combined. Garnish with a carrot top.

Bone Broth

Todd Schulte, Uncommon Stock, Kansas City, Missouri

Makes 2 to 3 quarts

5 pounds grass-fed beef bones (combination of knuckle, shank, and marrow bones)

3 to 4 quarts (12 to 16 cups) cold water

1 large onion (yellow or white)

1 large carrot

1 large leek

4 cloves garlic

1 tablespoon whole black peppercorns

12 sprigs fresh thyme

12 sprigs fresh Italian parsley

2 tablespoons unfiltered apple cider vinegar

Beef bone broth is like an echo of steaks past: It's not overly meaty, but it's clearly not vegetarian. It's best to think of this as the base layer for soups, sauces, or drinking broth. Then you can add salt or different spices to finish what you started in the slow cooker.

//

Place the bones in a 6-quart slow cooker. Cover them with the water. Turn the temperature to low.

Let the bones simmer for 20 hours. Peel and roughly chop the onion, carrot, and leek into chunks or coins. Add the onion, carrot, and leek to the cooker. Peel and smash the garlic cloves and crack the peppercorns with the flat side of your knife. Add the garlic and pepper to the pot, along with the thyme, parsley, and vinegar. Remove the broth from the cooker 24 hours after you started.

Place a large metal bowl or pot beneath a fine-mesh strainer or colander and ladle in the stock. You're going to strain the stock again. Line the strainer with a slightly damp coffee filter (#6) and add the stock.

(continued)

Bone Broth (continued)

After the second pass, fill your sink with cold water and ice and submerge the metal container with stock in the ice bath. Stir the stock every 15 minutes to help release heat. At the same time, you can drain some water and add more ice. Once your food is 40°F, it's safe to place the bowl or pot of stock in your fridge. Store in an airtight container for 2 to 4 days. If you want to freeze the stock, pour it into a freezer-safe container with the lid off. Leave ½ inch to 1-inch of space to allow for the stock to expand. After 6 hours in the freezer, place the lid on your stock and label it with the date it's frozen. You'll want to use it within 4 months.

TO ENJOY AS A DRINKING BROTH: There are lots of ways to garnish it. Three good choices are freshly grated ginger, turmeric, and star anise. Start with a ratio of ¼ teaspoon of any to 8 ounces (1 cup) of hot bone broth. Add a pinch of salt and let the broth steep for at least 10 minutes; add more spices if needed. If your store doesn't stock fresh turmeric, then a local Vietnamese or Asian specialty market is a good bet.

Grilled Corn, Black Bean & Quinoa Salad

Serves 4 to 6

3 ears corn (roughly 1½ cups kernels or frozen corn)

1 cup quinoa

Dash of olive oil

2 cups Bone Broth (page 38)

¼ teaspoon kosher salt, plus more as needed

¼ cup finely diced red onion

1½ large limes

1 (15-ounce) can black beans

½ cup finely chopped fresh cilantro

1 jalapeño (optional)

1 large avocado (optional)

Freshly ground black pepper

Hot sauce (optional)

This is the salad that you can be known for bringing to picnics and parties. It can come together in 30 minutes, but it has the depth of flavor and bright citrus to make it more complex. You can sub in water or The Roots Stock (page xviii) if you want to make this dish vegetarian/vegan.

//

When grilling fresh corn, shuck and clean the ears. Grill until cooked through, about 10 minutes, turning them every few minutes. This will get you a little bit of char, which works great with this salad. Set the corn aside on a plate to cool.

Once the corn is cool, use the method I first saw on Food52. Lay each cob flat on a cutting board and slice the right side first, moving a sharp knife slowly from the top of the cob to the bottom. Rotate the corn 90 degrees and repeat three times. Add the kernels to the large serving bowl you'll be using for the quinoa. Set aside.

(continued)

Grilled Corn, Black Bean & Quinoa Salad (continued)

Place the quinoa in a fine-mesh strainer and rinse several times with cold water. Toss the quinoa with your hand and press it into the strainer to help it drain. In order to dry the quinoa out fully, you can add a dash of olive oil to the bottom of a medium saucepan. Turn the heat to medium-high and place the quinoa in the pan. Stir it frequently for 1 minute, then add the broth and ¼ teaspoon kosher salt.

Bring the liquid in the pan to a rolling boil. Once it's boiling, cover the pan and turn the heat to low. Let it sit on the heat for 15 minutes.

While the quinoa is cooking, place the onion in a small bowl. Juice 1 lime and add the juice to the bowl with the onions—this will tone down the raw onion. Set aside. Drain and rinse the black beans. Place them in a serving bowl. If you're using frozen corn, here's where you defrost it and then add it to the serving bowl with the cilantro.

If you're adding a jalapeño, cut off the tip and stand the chile upright with the stem up. Slice from the top, curving the blade slightly in as you chop down. Rotate the jalapeño and keep slicing. Discard the stem and seeds. Remove any seeds stuck to the flesh. Then finely dice the jalapeño and add it to your serving bowl.

If you're adding an avocado, cut it in half, remove the pit, and scoop out the flesh. Cut it into ¼-inch cubes and add to the serving bowl.

After the 15 minutes are up, remove the quinoa from the heat and let it rest for 5 additional minutes. Keep the pot covered.

Remove the pot lid and fluff the quinoa with a fork. Add it to the serving bowl, which already has your beans, corn, and cilantro (and avocado and jalapeño if you're using), along with the red onion and lime juice. Season to taste with salt and pepper. Add a dash or two of hot sauce if you like.

You can serve this salad warm. If that's the case, add the additional juice of ½ lime and toss before serving. If you want to serve it cold, tightly wrap the top of your serving bowl with plastic wrap and place in the refrigerator for at least an hour.

When it's time to serve the cold salad, add the juice of ½ lime and additional salt and pepper if needed.

Orange & Guajillo Chile Turkey Stock

Todd Schulte, Uncommon Stock, Kansas City, Missouri

Makes 4 quarts

18- to 20-pound turkey carcass

1 gallon water

2 quarts (8 cups) ice cubes

1 large onion (yellow or white)

1 large carrot

1 large leek

4 cloves garlic

6 guajillo chiles

1 cup dried orange peel

1 bay leaf

1 tablespoon kosher salt

A touch of sweet and a touch of heat solve the most common post-Thanksgiving problem—how do you keep eating turkey without blowing past your turkey tolerance? The burnt-umber stock dazzles with the aroma and flavor of orange, so you'll drink it straight even as you're searching for the awl following your Thanksgiving dinner.

//

Place the turkey carcass in a large stockpot. Pour in the water and ice cubes. Turn the heat to medium-high. Peel and chop the onion, carrot, and leek into 1-inch chunks. Peel and smash the garlic. Tear the guajillo chiles into 6 or 8 pieces. Add the onion, carrot, leek, garlic, and chiles to the pot, along with the orange peel, bay leaf, and salt.

When the surface starts to become agitated, turn the heat down to medium-low and simmer for 4 hours.

(continued)

Orange & Guajillo Chile Turkey Stock (continued)

Remove the stockpot from the heat. Place a large metal bowl or pot beneath a fine-mesh strainer or colander and ladle in the stock. You're going to strain the stock again. Line the strainer with a slightly damp coffee filter (#6) and add the stock. After the second pass, fill your sink with cold water and ice and submerge the metal container with stock in the ice bath. Stir the stock every 15 minutes to help release heat. At the same time, you can drain some water and add more ice.

Once your food is 40°F, it's safe to place the bowl or pot of stock in your fridge. Store in an airtight container for 2 to 4 days. If you want to freeze the stock, pour it into a freezer-safe container with the lid off. Leave ½ inch to 1 inch of space to allow for the stock to expand. After 6 hours in the freezer, place the lid on your stock and label it with the date it's frozen. You'll want to use it within 4 months.

TO ENJOY AS A DRINKING BROTH: Pour 1 cup of hot stock into a mug or French press. Add 2 pencil-thin strips of orange zest and steep for 10 minutes. Remove the zest. Salt to taste. The stock's sweetness could also be offset by a few drops of Cholula hot sauce or brightened up with chopped parsley and whole black peppercorns.

Braised Short Ribs

Serves 4

3 pounds bone-in short ribs

2 tablespoons vegetable oil

Kosher salt and freshly ground black pepper

1 medium yellow onion

4 cloves garlic

2 large carrots

2 celery stalks

½ cup red wine

1 tablespoon balsamic vinegar

3 cups Orange & Guajillo Chile Turkey Stock (page 43)

2 sprigs fresh rosemary

2 sprigs fresh thyme

Polenta (optional)

Mashed potatoes (optional)

Crusty bread (optional)

You deserve some braise. These tender short ribs announce their deliciousness by filling the kitchen with a primal call to eat. The orange in the stock cuts through the richness, but this dish is still a pot of luxury. Serve these over mashed potatoes, polenta, or with crusty bread—anything that lets you soak up the deep, savory gravy.

//

Preheat the oven to 325°F. Rub the short ribs with the vegetable oil, then season with salt and pepper. (You can toss them in a mixing bowl to achieve the same effect.)

You want there to be space between the ribs, so you'll likely have to cook them in two batches. If that's the case, try to cook ribs of equal width so they sear at the same rate. After you brown the short ribs, set aside on a plate.

Place an oven-safe pot or Dutch oven on the stove and turn the heat to medium-high. Place the short ribs in the pot and sear for 1 to 2 minutes on all four sides. (Just a heads-up: Your kitchen will get a little smoky.)

While you're browning the short ribs, peel the onion, garlic, and carrots. Cut the ends off the onion and slice it vertically into $\frac{1}{8}$-inch-thick slices. Cut those slices in half horizontally. Place the onions in a medium-size bowl. Mince the garlic and add to the onion. Cut the carrots and celery stalks into 1-inch-long chunks of roughly equal width. Add to the bowl and set aside.

When the short ribs are browned, add the vegetables to the drippings in the pot. Turn the heat down to medium and stir with a wooden spoon or spatula every 2 minutes or so. Cook for 6 to 8 minutes, until the onions soften and begin to get some color.

Add the wine and vinegar and raise the heat to medium-high. Scrape up any browned bits from the bottom of the pan with a wooden spoon or whisk. Bring the mixture to a boil for 1 to 2 minutes, letting the wine reduce slightly. Add the turkey stock, rosemary, and thyme, and let the contents of a pot come to a steady simmer. You want bubbles, not froth.

If the surface gets too hot too quickly, you can skim away the froth. Once the broth is at a simmer, cover it and place in the oven.

Bake for $2\frac{1}{2}$ hours, until the meat is falling off the bone. Remove the pot from the oven and place on a trivet for 20 minutes. Skim off any fat from the cooking liquid with a spoon or ladle. Discard the fat.

Use tongs to place a short rib or two over polenta or mashed potatoes or serve with crusty bread. Spoon some sauce over the ribs, add a vegetable or two if you want (the carrots will be soft but tasty), and serve.

Tortilla Turkey Soup

Serves 6

1½ pounds boneless, skinless chicken thighs

2 tablespoons olive oil

1 medium yellow onion, roughly chopped

4 cloves garlic, roughly chopped

1 tablespoon ancho chile powder

1 (14.5-ounce) can diced tomatoes

½ teaspoon cumin

2 quarts (8 cups) Orange & Guajillo Chile Turkey Stock (page 43)

Kosher salt

1 large lime, cut into 8 slices, for serving

Blue and yellow corn tortilla chips, for serving

1 large avocado (optional)

2 cups (8 ounces) crumbled queso fresco (or shredded mild cheddar cheese)

½ cup sour cream

This is a cozy soup. The guajillo chile in the stock gives you warmth without heat beneath a creamy blanket of cheese. The tortilla chips add a nice bit of crunch, and the chicken gives more body to the broth. Treat this soup like a taco bar and let your dinner guests doctor it up with avocado or hot sauce.

///

Place the chicken thighs in a pot big enough so they can lay flat on the bottom without overlapping. Add enough water to completely cover the chicken. Turn the heat to high and bring the water to a boil. Cover partially and turn the heat to medium until the water is a steady simmer. Cook the chicken for roughly 30 minutes, until a fork easily pierces the tender meat and can remove it from the bone.

Remove the chicken to a flat-bottomed bowl to cool. Once cool enough to handle, shred the chicken with two forks or your fingers.

Add the olive oil to a large stockpot or Dutch oven and turn the heat to medium-high. Add the onion and garlic to the pot and cook for 3 to 4 minutes. When the onion starts to become translucent, add the ancho chile powder. Cook for another 4 minutes, stirring frequently to keep the onions from browning and to evenly coat them with the chile.

Place the tomatoes and their juices in a blender. Add the onions and garlic, turning the heat to low on the pot so any bits stuck to the bottom don't burn. Blend the tomatoes, onions, and garlic until smooth, 2 to 3 minutes.

Pour the blended mixture back into the pot and bring the heat back to medium-high. Add the cumin. Let the mixture thicken and darken slightly over 10 to 12 minutes. Stir occasionally. Add the stock to the pot and simmer on medium or medium-low for 15 to 20 minutes. If the pot is steaming, it's too hot. Taste and season with salt if needed.

Place the lime in a small bowl on the table along with the tortilla chips. If you're adding avocado, cut it in half, remove the pit, and scoop out the flesh. Cut it into roughly ¼-inch cubes. You can place them in a bowl or use as a garnish for the soup.

Place even amounts of the chicken in the bottom of the bowls and then ladle the soup on top of the chicken. Add about ¼ cup cheese and a big dollop of sour cream to each bowl. Serve immediately and tell your guests to crumble as many tortilla chips as they like and sprinkle them on the soup.

Lemongrass Chicken Stock

Todd Schulte, Uncommon Stock, Kansas City, Missouri

Makes 2 to 2½ quarts

1 (3½-pound) chicken carcass

2 pounds chicken wings

3½ quarts (14 cups) cold water, divided

2 quarts (8 cups) ice cubes

12 sprigs fresh Italian parsley

1 large carrot

1 large leek

1 large yellow onion

1 teaspoon whole black peppercorns

12 cloves garlic

4 bay leaves

6 stalks lemongrass

1½ teaspoons kosher salt

Fresh ginger (optional)

This is what would happen if a Jewish grandmother and a Taiwanese grandmother sat next to each other on a bus and decided to make a stock together. It's got this bright punch from the lemongrass and the warm comfort that is at the base of every great bowl of chicken noodle soup.

//

Place the chicken carcass and chicken wings in a Dutch oven or large stockpot. Add 2½ quarts of the water and the ice cubes.

Rinse the parsley and add it to the pot. Peel the carrot, leek, and onion. Dry the vegetables and roughly chop them into large chunks. Pulse the vegetables in a food processor until you have pea-size pieces. Add them to the pot.

Place the whole peppercorns on a cutting board. Crush the peppercorns by holding the side of a blade over the peppercorns and pushing down until you hear a crack. Remove the skin from the 12 garlic cloves and use the same technique to smash them. Add the peppercorns, garlic, bay leaves, lemongrass stalks, and salt to the pot.

Turn the heat to medium-high for 20 to 25 minutes, until the surface just starts to become agitated—it will appear almost shimmery. Then, turn the heat down to medium-low and simmer for 5 hours. You want a slow simmer, where the bubbles are just breaking rather than rolling across the surface. The chicken should cook, but not be breaking into pieces. If the meat breaks off the bones, it will muddy the stock.

After 3 hours, add the remaining 1 quart of cold water if the water line has gone down by more than 1 inch. (Look at the side of the pot and compare the original water line, marked by the stock residue, to the level of the stock.)

Remove the stockpot from the heat. Place a large metal bowl or pot beneath a fine-mesh strainer or colander and ladle in the stock. You're going to strain the stock again. Line the strainer with a slightly damp coffee filter (#6) and add the stock. After the second pass, fill your sink with cold water and ice and submerge the metal container with stock in the ice bath. Stir the stock every 15 minutes to help release heat. At the same time, you can drain some water and add more ice. Once your food is 40°F, it's safe to place the bowl or pot of stock in your fridge. Store in an airtight container for 2 to 4 days. If you want to freeze the stock, pour it into a freezer-safe container with the lid off. Leave ½ inch to 1 inch of space to allow for the stock to expand. After 6 hours in the freezer, place the lid on your stock and label it with the date it's frozen. You'll want to use it within 4 months.

TO ENJOY AS A DRINKING BROTH: Pour 1 cup of hot stock into a mug or French press. Add 3 stalks of lemongrass and steep for 10 minutes. Remove the lemongrass. Salt to taste. You could also steep 2 quarter-size slices or coins of fresh ginger in the same fashion. For those who want heat, opt for a drizzle of garlic-chili oil.

Wednesday White Bean Soup

Serves 4 to 6

SOUP

2 tablespoons olive oil

5 slices thick-cut maple bacon

1 small yellow onion, chopped

1 red bell pepper, seeded and chopped

3 cloves garlic, minced

2 carrots, peeled and chopped

2 celery stalks, chopped

4 sprigs fresh rosemary, stemmed

2 (15-ounce) cans cannellini beans

3 cups Lemongrass Chicken Stock (page 50)

½ cup plus 2 tablespoons freshly grated Parmigiano-Reggiano cheese

1 tablespoon freshly squeezed lemon juice (optional)

Kosher salt and freshly ground black pepper

SOURDOUGH CROUTONS

1 loaf sourdough bread

Extra-virgin olive oil, for drizzling

2 tablespoons freshly grated Parmigiano-Reggiano cheese

This soup is for when your weekly meal plan has fallen apart. In other words: It's Wednesday and you need dinner put together in short order. The bacon lends some smokiness to the soup, but it's a creamy winner even if you don't have bacon on hand. It also freezes well if you find yourself in a pickle the following Wednesday.

//

Preheat the oven to 400°F. Place the olive oil in a Dutch oven or large stockpot and turn the heat to medium-high. Add the bacon to the oil and cook for 5 minutes per side, until brown but not blackened. Remove the bacon to a baking sheet. Finish cooking it in the oven for 5 to 10 minutes. When it's done, set aside on a paper towel–lined plate to drain. Lower the oven temperature to 375°F.

Add the onion, red pepper, garlic, carrots, and celery to the pot and sauté for 10 minutes, until the carrots start to feel soft. Add the rosemary stems to the pot, reserving the leaves. Drain and rinse the cannellini beans and add to the pot, along with the stock and cheese. Purée with a handheld blender until smooth. Bring to a boil on high heat, then lower the heat to medium-low. Cover and simmer for at least 20 minutes.

To make the croutons, cut the sourdough bread into ½-inch cubes. You should have about 4 cups. Place them in a medium-size bowl and drizzle olive oil and the cheese over the top. Toss the bread cubes to make sure they're evenly coated. Spread in a single layer on a baking sheet and bake for 20 to 30 minutes, until the bread is crispy and starting to turn golden. Toss them halfway through baking.

Chop the bacon into bits and set aside in a bowl. When the croutons are ready, taste the soup and season with salt and pepper. Ladle the soup into bowls, add a few drops of lemon juice to the top, if using, along with the croutons, rosemary leaves, and bacon bits.

You can store the soup in an airtight container in the fridge for up to 2 days. This soup can also be made a day ahead of time.

Pretty Pink Pasta

Serves 4 to 6

3 or 4 medium beets

2 tablespoons plus 2 teaspoons
olive oil, divided

¼ cup walnuts (optional)

2 medium yellow onions

1 clove garlic

Kosher salt and freshly ground
black pepper

2 cups Lemongrass Chicken Stock
(page 50)

10 ounces farfalle

4 ounces goat cheese

¼ cup finely chopped
fresh Italian parsley

½ teaspoon freshly squeezed
lemon juice (optional)

½ teaspoon crushed red pepper
(optional)

It's a splash of color or a great bit of branding for those with toddlers, but Pretty Pink Pasta, as it is known in my house, is a winner of a dish. The sweetness of the beets and onions is nicely balanced by the greens and chicken stock, meaning this is not just a novelty, but also a regular addition to your late-summer rotation.

//

Preheat the oven to 375°F. Remove the beet greens and separate the leaves from the stems. Discard the stems. Rinse the leaves, chop them into 1-inch strips, and set aside. Scrub the beets well, pat them dry, and then lightly coat them in 1 teaspoon olive oil. Wrap individually in aluminum foil and place on a baking sheet. Bake for 45 to 60 minutes, until a fork easily pierces the skin. Let the beets cool, then use a paper towel to remove the skins. Roughly chop the beets, about the size of breakfast potatoes. Set aside.

If using the walnuts, decrease the oven temperature to 350°F. Place the walnuts in a single layer on a baking sheet and bake until lightly toasted. Check after 6 minutes. (It will likely be closer to 8 to 10 minutes.) Remove from the heat and let cool on a plate.

(continued)

Pretty Pink Pasta (continued)

Place 2 tablespoons of olive oil in a deep skillet or saucepan over medium-high heat. While the oil warms, peel and finely chop the onions and mince the garlic. Add the onions to the oil and sauté for 10 minutes, until they begin to turn golden. Then add the garlic and lower the heat to medium. Cook the onions and garlic for an additional 30 minutes, stirring every 6 to 8 minutes, until the onions are brown and caramelized. Add the beet greens with the remaining 1 teaspoon of olive oil. Cover the pan and let cook for 3 minutes. Then add the chopped beets and season with salt and pepper. Turn the heat to low.

After the onions have been cooking for 20 minutes, place the stock and 1 cup of water in a medium pot and bring to a boil. Add the farfalle and, based on the pasta package's instructions, cook until it's al dente.

Drain the pasta in a colander, reserving the pasta water. Add ½ cup of the pasta water to the skillet with the onion, garlic, beet greens, and beets, along with the goat cheese. Stir until the cheese is blended and then add the farfalle, another ½ cup of pasta water, and the parsley.

Stir gently, making sure the beets and greens are well distributed and the pasta is a uniform pink color. If the sauce is turning to paste, add a few table-spoons of pasta water until you have the consistency you like.

Place the pasta into bowls and then garnish with a few drops of lemon juice and crushed red pepper if you like.

Cremini Mushroom & Thyme Stock

Todd Schulte, Uncommon Stock, Kansas City, Missouri

Makes 3 quarts

**16 cloves garlic
(1½ to 2 heads), divided**

1 teaspoon olive oil

4 quarts (16 cups) cold water, divided

**1 ounce dried mushrooms
(blend of porcini and portobello)**

1 teaspoon whole black peppercorns

12 sprigs fresh Italian parsley

12 sprigs fresh thyme

1 pound cremini mushrooms

1 large leek

1 large carrot

1 large yellow onion

4 bay leaves

1½ teaspoons kosher salt

This is why pigs go find truffles. You'll bury your nose in the pot for the deep, warm embrace of this earthy stock. A big pop of thyme gives way to this silky umami quality. Find your inner hobbit and feel like you've just spent the afternoon foraging when you create a hearty elixir that has the echo of the land without being gritty.

///

Preheat the oven to 400°F. In a small bowl, trim off the top of the garlic, about ¼ inch. Break the head of garlic into individual cloves, leaving the skin on and the cloves intact. Grab 4 cloves and set the rest aside. Combine the olive oil with the 4 cloves in a bowl and gently toss it until evenly coated. Wrap the cloves in a foil pouch and place in the oven. After 25 minutes, begin to check for doneness. The garlic is ready when it's golden brown and easily pierced with a knife. Set the cloves aside to cool.

In a small saucepan, bring 1 quart of water to a boil. As soon as the first bubbles break on the surface, remove the pan from the heat. Add the dried mushrooms and let them soak for 30 minutes.

Place the whole peppercorns on a cutting board. Crush the peppercorns by holding the side of a blade over them and pushing down until you hear a crack. Set the peppercorns aside in a small bowl. Remove the skin from the reserved 12 garlic cloves and use the same technique to smash them. Add them to the bowl with the peppercorns.

Rinse the parsley and thyme. Pat the herbs dry with a paper towel and set aside. Wash the cremini mushrooms. Peel the leek, carrot, and onion. Dry the vegetables and roughly chop them into large chunks. Pulse the vegetables in a food processor until you have pea-size pieces.

Place the chopped vegetables in an 8-quart pot or Dutch oven. Add the remaining 3 quarts of cold water to the pot. Peel the skin off the roasted garlic and add it to the pot. Then add the smashed garlic gloves, cracked black pepper, parsley, thyme, bay leaves, and salt.

Turn the heat to medium-high for 15 to 20 minutes, until the surface just starts to become agitated—it will appear almost shimmery. Turn the heat down to medium-low. You want a slow simmer, where the bubbles are just breaking rather than rolling across the surface.

After another 10 minutes, add the soaked mushrooms. Reserve the mushroom soaking water and pour it through a strainer to catch any sediment, and then add to the pot. Keep the pot on the stove for another 45 minutes and then remove it from the heat.

Place a large metal bowl or pot beneath a fine-mesh strainer or colander and ladle in the stock. You're going to strain the stock again. Line the strainer with a slightly damp coffee filter (#6) and add the stock. After the second pass, fill your sink with cold water and ice and submerge the metal container with stock in the ice bath. Stir the stock every 15 minutes to help release heat. At the same time, you can drain some water and add more ice. Once your food is 40°F, it's safe to place the bowl or pot of stock in your fridge. Store in an airtight container for 2 to 4 days. If you want to freeze the stock, pour it into a freezer-safe container with the lid off. Leave ½ inch to 1 inch of space to allow for the stock to expand. After 6 hours in the freezer, place the lid on your stock and label it with the date it's frozen. You'll want to use it within 4 months.

TO ENJOY AS A DRINKING BROTH: Pour 1 cup of hot stock into a mug or French press. Add a sprig of thyme (or rosemary) and 2 pencil-thin strips of lemon zest. Steep for 10 minutes. Remove the herbs and zest. Salt to taste. If you want a bit of heat, you can add a few red pepper flakes (a little goes a long way) and rosemary. You could also opt for a splash of soy sauce and sesame oil, a pinch of ground ginger, and Sriracha to make a spicy Asian broth.

Mushroom Risotto

Serves 3 or 4

2 tablespoons unsalted butter

1 tablespoon olive oil

1 small yellow onion, finely diced

1 small shallot, finely diced

3 cloves garlic, minced

½ teaspoon salt, divided

Pinch of freshly ground black pepper

1¼ cups Arborio rice

5 cups Cremini Mushroom & Thyme Stock (page 58)

¾ cup freshly grated Parmigiano-Reggiano cheese, divided

6 sprigs fresh thyme (optional)

Zest strips of ½ large lemon (optional)

This risotto is unfair. It shows you a deep, rich world that you can only reach with homemade stock. Earthy and hearty, the mushroom risotto has a blooming warmth and creaminess from (admittedly) a lot of cheese. If you need to sell it to someone under five years old, just take the party line from our house and call it "cheesy rice." It's easy to double this if you're having folks over for dinner.

//

In a medium saucepan, melt the butter and warm the oil over medium-high heat. Once the butter is completely melted, add the onion, shallot, and garlic to the pan along with ¼ teaspoon of salt and the pepper.

Cook the vegetables in the pot for 3 to 5 minutes, until the onions are translucent. If they start to brown or blacken, turn down the heat. Add the rice and let it cook for 4 to 5 minutes, stirring every 15 to 20 seconds. When the rice is a uniform tan color, add 1 cup of the mushroom stock. Turn the heat down to medium.

(continued)

Mushroom Risotto *(continued)*

Stir every 2 minutes, folding a spatula or wooden spoon under the rice to make sure it's not sticking to the bottom of the pan. Allow the stock to be completely absorbed, about 10 minutes, before adding the second cup. If you have a lot of steam or the stock is absorbed rapidly, turn the heat down to medium-low.

Add a third cup of mushroom stock and continue stirring. Divide the cheese into three ¼-cup portions. Set aside. After another 10 to 12 minutes, add the fourth cup of stock, along with ¼ cup of cheese, the remaining ¼ teaspoon of salt, and another pinch of pepper.

When the stock is absorbed, add the fifth cup of stock. Start stirring every minute. Five minutes later, add another ¼ cup of Parmigiano-Reggiano. Put on the radio or grab a glass of wine because now you're with the pot until the end. Stir every 30 seconds and taste the risotto for the first time. Add more salt and pepper if needed.

You're looking for the creamy rice to be slightly firm, but not crunchy. When you plate it, the rice will move like a glacier—slow enough to see, but only if you spend a while watching it. When the texture is right, serve it in deep dinner plates. If you like, garnish with thyme and two thin strips of lemon zest. Bring the remaining ¼ cup of cheese to the table for serving.

Mushroom Bourguignonne

Serves 2 to 4

1 medium yellow onion

½ pound white button mushrooms (or cremini)

½ pound portobello mushroom caps

3 tablespoons unsalted butter, divided

1 tablespoon extra-virgin olive oil

1 large carrot

2 cloves garlic

1 small shallot

½ teaspoon coriander seeds

Kosher salt and freshly ground black pepper

½ cup red wine

2 tablespoons tomato paste

½ teaspoon balsamic vinegar

2 tablespoons all-purpose flour

2 cups Cremini Mushroom & Thyme Stock (page 58)

2 sprigs fresh thyme

1 bay leaf

1 cup Bone Broth Quinoa from Grilled Corn, Black Bean & Quinoa Salad (page 41)

Butter, wine, and decadence: This is the sumptuous kind of vegetarian dish that will give even ardent carnivores pause. It's got the depth and warmth that beef bourguignonne promises without having to make a day of it in the kitchen.

//

Peel and dice the onion into ¼-inch pieces. Set aside in a small bowl. Rinse the mushrooms well and pat dry. Remove the stems, if attached, and chop the mushrooms into roughly 1-inch cubes. (It's more important that they're roughly the same size and big enough not to crumble than the size is exact.)

Place 2 tablespoons of the butter and the olive oil in a heavy-bottomed pot over medium-high heat. Add the mushrooms and cook for 3 to 4 minutes, until the mushrooms brown but not to the point where they're releasing a lot of liquid.

Remove the mushrooms from the heat and set aside on a plate. Add the onion to the pot and cook for 10 minutes. While the onion is cooking, peel the carrot, garlic, and shallot. Chop the carrot into ¼-inch cubes and mince the garlic and shallot. Add them to the pot. Cook for another 10 minutes. Crack the coriander seeds with the point or flat side of your knife. Add to the pot with a pinch of salt and pepper.

Add the wine and raise the heat to high. Let the wine bubble for 1 minute, scraping up any browned bits from the bottom of the pan. Then add the mushrooms and cook for another 1 to 2 minutes, until the wine is a very thin layer at the bottom of the pan. Add the tomato paste and vinegar and cook for another 3 minutes on medium-high—you're looking for the consistency of a gravy. Stir the vegetables consistently but gently. Add the flour and stir for another 1 to 2 minutes, until the vegetables are evenly coated and you don't feel any lumps.

Pour in the stock and add the thyme and bay leaf. Raise the heat to medium-high and let the pot come to a boil. Turn the heat down to medium or medium-low and keep the pot at an active simmer for 20 minutes. You want rolling bubbles to let the sauce start to reduce.

Remove the bay leaf and thyme sprigs. Season with salt and pepper to taste. Serve over the quinoa.

Shrimp & Fine Herb Stock

Todd Schulte, Uncommon Stock, Kansas City, Missouri

Makes 3 to 3½ quarts

1 pound shrimp shells

1 tablespoon extra-virgin olive oil

6 cloves garlic

1 large carrot

1 large leek

1 large onion (yellow or white)

1 small fennel bulb

2 (14.5-ounce) cans diced tomatoes

1½ teaspoons salt

1 gallon cold water

1 cup chopped fresh chervil (French parsley)

1 cup chopped fresh chives

1 cup chopped fresh tarragon

This stock gets its lovely pink color from the shrimp—it's beautiful stock. "You should taste the sea," says Todd Schulte after dipping a spoon into a fresh batch. And you do get the comforting undercurrent of chowder and mussels on the breeze, even if that breeze comes in through the open garage doors of Schulte's kitchen in landlocked Kansas City, Missouri.

//

Rinse the shrimp shells if they haven't been cleaned. Add the olive oil to a stockpot and turn the heat to medium-high. Place the shrimp shells in the pot and cook for 4 minutes, until they start to get pink.

Peel the skin and smash the garlic cloves with the side of your knife. Set aside. Peel and chop the carrot and leek into 1-inch pieces. Peel and dice the onion. Cut off the stalks and peel the fennel bulb. Chop into 1-inch pieces.

Add the carrot, leek, onion, and fennel to the pot. Mix them in evenly with the shrimp shells in order to coat the vegetables with oil, but not to change their color or caramelize them. After a minute or two, add the 2 cans of tomatoes with juices, smashed garlic, salt, and cold water.

(continued)

Shrimp & Fine Herb Stock (continued)

When the surface starts to become agitated, turn the heat down to medium-low and simmer for 25 minutes. Wash and chop the chervil, chives, and tarragon. Add them to the top of the stock after you lower the heat and cover the pot.

Remove the stockpot from the heat. Place a large metal bowl or pot beneath a fine-mesh strainer or colander and ladle in the stock. You're going to strain the stock again. Line the strainer with a slightly damp coffee filter (#6) and add the stock. After the second pass, fill your sink with cold water and ice and submerge the metal container with the stock in the ice bath. Stir the stock every 15 minutes to help release heat. At the same time, you can drain some water and add more ice. Once your food is 40°F, it's safe to place the bowl or pot of stock in your fridge. Store in an airtight container for 2 to 4 days. If you want to freeze the stock, pour it into a freezer-safe container with the lid off. Leave ½ inch to 1 inch of space to allow for the stock to expand. After 6 hours in the freezer, place the lid on your stock and label it with the date it's frozen. You'll want to use it within 4 months.

TO ENJOY AS A DRINKING BROTH: Pour 1 cup of hot stock into a mug or French press. Add a few sprigs of the chervil, tarragon, and chives, and steep for 10 minutes. Remove the herbs. Salt to taste. You could also steep 2 quarter-size pieces of fresh ginger, or finely chop green onions and add a splash of dry sherry or rice wine to round out the stock's sweetness.

Mussels in Shrimp Broth

Serves 4 as an appetizer
or 2 for dinner

2 pounds mussels

1 large shallot

3 cloves garlic

2 tablespoons unsalted butter

1 (14.5-ounce) can diced tomatoes

1½ cups Shrimp & Fine Herb Stock
(page 66)

½ cup dry white wine

1 baguette

1 large lemon

1 cup chopped fresh Italian parsley

You'll tell yourself that you're done, even as you find yourself reaching for another crust of bread to dredge through the beautiful light red sauce that only took you minutes to make. And you can take this recipe in different directions, adding a touch of red pepper flakes or chorizo to spice up the piquant dish.

//

Place the mussels in a strainer and rinse well with cold water. You want to remove any grit. Discard any that have cracked shells. If a mussel is slightly open, tap it gently on the counter. If it closes, put it back in the strainer. If it stays open, throw it away, for alas, that mussel has died. Check to see if the beards—brown strings—are still attached. If they are, pinch with your thumb and forefinger and pull. This is just for taste—mussels are not hipsters, hence the beards don't belong.

(continued)

Mussels in Shrimp Broth (continued)

Peel and mince the shallot and garlic. Place the butter in a wide, shallow saucepan or Dutch oven and melt on medium-high heat. Cook the shallot and garlic for 2 minutes, until you start to smell the garlic. You don't want either the shallots or garlic to brown. Add the tomatoes with their juices to the pot, as well as the mussels. Pour the stock and wine over the top of the mussels.

Cover the pot and let cook for 5 minutes. Grab a pot holder and shake the pot gently about halfway through to make sure all the mussels get cooked. While the mussels are cooking, slice your baguette, cut your lemon into wedges and rinse and chop the parsley leaves. Set the parsley aside. Bring the baguette slices and lemon to the table. While you're there, place a trivet down for the pot of mussels along with a few bowls for empty shells

After 5 minutes have passed, remove the lid to the pan. A majority of the mussels should be open. If not, put the top back on and steam for an additional 2 minutes.

Take the pot off the heat and, with a slotted spoon or tongs, remove any mussels that haven't opened. Sprinkle the chopped parsley over the top of the mussels. Place the pot on the trivet and serve immediately.

⁝ Seafood Stew ⁝

Serves 6

1 small yellow onion

1 large leek

2 large carrots

2 stalks celery

1½ cups diced red potatoes

½ cup yellow corn (fresh or frozen)

1 slice slab bacon

1 tablespoon unsalted butter (optional)

Kosher salt and freshly ground black pepper

1 pound large shrimp (26 to 30 count size)

½ pound cod (or haddock or monkfish)

½ pound lump crabmeat (or scallops)

¼ cup all-purpose flour

4 cups (1 quart) Shrimp & Fine Herb Stock (page 66)

2 tablespoons freshly squeezed lemon juice (about 1 small lemon)

1 cup chopped fresh Italian parsley, for garnish

½ cup chopped fresh chives, for garnish

Oyster crackers, for serving

This stew falls somewhere between cioppino and chowder—it's hearty and silky, even without cream. Feel free to swap in other shellfish, bivalves, or fish. Just avoid delicate, flaky fish, as they'll disintegrate in your stew.

///

Peel and dice the onion, leek, and carrots into roughly ½-inch cubes. Rinse the celery and dice to the same size. Place the onion, leek, carrots, celery, potatoes, and corn in a bowl.

Chop the bacon into ¼-inch squares. Place the bacon in a large, heavy-bottomed pot or Dutch oven on medium-high heat. Let brown for 4 to 6 minutes, flipping with a wooden spoon to keep it from sticking. If the bacon starts to turn black, turn down your heat slightly.

Add the vegetables to the pot. If they soak up all the fat released by the bacon or you feel like they're sticking, add the butter. Turn the heat to medium-low and cook for 15 minutes, stirring every few minutes, until the potatoes begin to soften. Add a few pinches of salt and pepper.

While the vegetables are cooking, rinse, peel, and devein the shrimp. Save the shells in a freezer-safe, resealable plastic bag to use for shrimp stock in the future. Slice the shrimp in half with a vertical cut and place in a bowl. Chop the cod and crab into 1½- to 2-inch chunks, just big enough to hang over a large soupspoon. Add to the shrimp and set aside.

After the vegetables have been cooking for 15 minutes, add the flour and stir frequently for 2 to 3 minutes, until all the vegetables are evenly coated. Add the shrimp stock and lemon juice, and raise the heat to medium-high. Bring the stock to a boil. Once it's boiling, add the shrimp, cod, and crabmeat to the stock and cook for 8 to 10 minutes. Turn the heat down to medium-low—you want the surface to be at a steady simmer, with bubbles, not frothing.

The shrimp will turn pink, and the fish will turn opaque. You want everything to be just cooked, so it doesn't turn to mush in your guests' bowls.

Season the stew with salt and pepper and then ladle into bowls. If you like, garnish with chopped parsley and chives. Serve with oyster crackers.

Contributors

Alex Pope

Alex Pope is a chef and the owner of The Local Pig, a whole-animal butcher shop that focuses on local and sustainable meat production, in Kansas City, Missouri. Before opening a butcher shop, he worked at The American Restaurant and created a series of pop-up dinners under the name Vagabond. A native of Wisconsin and graduate of the Institute of Culinary Education, Pope was nominated as one of the People's Best New Chefs in the Midwest by *Food & Wine* magazine in 2011.

Patrick Ryan

As executive chef–owner of Port Fonda, Patrick Ryan is at the forefront of the culinary revolution in Kansas City, Missouri. He takes a simple, ingredient-focused approach to Mexican street food, melding authentic flavors with a farm-driven Midwestern sensibility. Ryan's passion for Mexican cuisine first developed from his relationship with the people, as he started working in the kitchen at a very young age alongside Mexican cooks. Ryan earned a bachelor's degree from the Western State College of Colorado (now known as Western State Colorado University), followed by a culinary degree at Le Cordon Bleu's Western Culinary Institute in Portland, Oregon. He then worked in Chicago under celebrated chef Rick Bayless at Frontera Grill and Topolobampo. A Kansas City native, Ryan returned to his hometown in 2010 to open the first iteration of Port Fonda, an underground restaurant in a vintage Airstream trailer, that summer. He went on to open the brick-and-mortar Port Fonda in summer 2012, seamlessly translating the fast-paced, uncensored, street-food mentality to a restaurant environment. He was nominated for *Food & Wine*'s People's Best New Chef award in 2013 and 2014 and, most recently, the James Beard Foundation's Best Chef: Midwest 2015.

Todd Schulte

Todd Schulte is the chef and co-owner of Genessee Royale Bistro and Uncommon Stock. After years of living and attending culinary college in Baltimore, Maryland, he traveled extensively and met his wife, Tracy Zinn. Schulte and Zinn decided to return to Kansas City to set their sights on their own design. After starting Kansas City's first soup home delivery, Happy Soup Eater, they decided to launch a small neighborhood hangout. In 2008, the husband-and-wife team opened Happy Gillis Cafe & Hangout, which was later featured on Food Network's *Diners, Drive-Ins, and Dives*.

In 2010, Schulte and Zinn opened a second restaurant, Genessee Royale Bistro, in Kansas City's Stockyards District located in the West Bottoms. Later, Schulte and partner Bill Haw rebranded the popular soup company as Uncommon Stock and currently distribute to high-end grocers and artisan markets. Schulte currently lives in Kansas City, Missouri, with his wife and daughters, Eden and Phoebe.

Arturo Vera-Felicie

Arturo Vera-Felicie was born in Puerto Rico and came to the continental United States in 1987. He joined the Marine Corps in 1999 and moved to Kansas City, Missouri, after a couple of tours overseas. He started in the service industry working the door at Buzzard Beach. He earned his first bartending award in 2009, winning the Greater Kansas City bartending competition, which is now known as the Paris of the Plains. He has spent the past five years developing bar programs for independently owned restaurants in Kansas City. He currently manages the beverage program at the Justus Drugstore in Smithville, Missouri.

Acknowledgments

The best part of every book is the chance to collaborate with talented people. And I was fortunate to have a lot of them on this project. My agent, Jonathan Lyons, is a dedicated advocate and true professional—I am very lucky in this regard.

And to you. Thank you for taking the time to pick up this book and read it. I hope that it serves you well in your kitchen and makes your world genuinely tastier and easier. Go get some stains on this thing already.

The crew at Andrews McMeel is a committed partner, and I'm glad we're in the same city. There's joy in playing for the hometown team. To everyone who worked on this book, thank you for your time and efforts on this endeavor's behalf. My editor, Jean Lucas, is wonderfully open and honest about what will make something better; Julie Barnes has lovely taste; and Maureen Sullivan made subtle and key improvements. The mistakes are mine, and I own them as such.

Stock, Broth & Bowl was built with the talents of three men. Chef/butcher Alex Pope provided stock recipes and the bones to cook them, and chef Todd Schulte literally threw open the garage doors of his commissary kitchen and helped to energize this project. Both gave freely and happily of their time and abilities. Mixologist Arturo Vera-Felicie dove behind the bar and stood in front of the stove to help shine a light on savory cocktails. As a bonus, chef Patrick Ryan of Port Fonda was quick to share a brilliant soup recipe that should be featured in everyone's summer rotation.

For the photo shoot, Ben Pieper and Anneka DeJong created a comforting environment and knocked out pictures that showed how pretty stock can be with the right person behind the camera. Food stylist Sarah Jane Hunt brought positivity and a deft touch, along with a kitchen marshal in Tammy Peek, an indefatigable cook with an eagle eye.

My family is simply the greatest. Abe and Charlotte, although you are now made mostly of pot roast, I appreciate you experimenting alongside your dad. To my wife, Kate, I sincerely apologize for making you eat marshmallows made with pork stock. Your willingness to try them for a second time on the next day is why it's true love.

Metric Conversions & Equivalents

TO CONVERT	MULTIPLY	TO CONVERT	MULTIPLY
Ounces to grams	Ounces by 28.35	Cups to milliliters	Cups by 236.59
Pounds to kilograms	Pounds by .454	Cups to liters	Cups by .236
Teaspoons to milliliters	Teaspoons by 4.93	Pints to liters	Pints by .473
Tablespoons to milliliters	Tablespoons by 14.79	Quarts to liters	Quarts by .946
Fluid ounces to milliliters	Fluid ounces by 29.57	Gallons to liters	Gallons by 3.785
		Inches to centimeters	Inches by 2.54

APPROXIMATE METRIC EQUIVALENTS

VOLUME

¼ teaspoon	1 milliliter
½ teaspoon	2.5 milliliters
¾ teaspoon	4 milliliters
1 teaspoon	5 milliliters
1¼ teaspoons	6 milliliters
1½ teaspoons	7.5 milliliters
1¾ teaspoons	8.5 milliliters
2 teaspoons	10 milliliters
1 tablespoon (½ fluid ounce)	15 milliliters
2 tablespoons (1 fluid ounce)	30 milliliters
¼ cup	60 milliliters
⅓ cup	80 milliliters
½ cup (4 fluid ounces)	120 milliliters
⅔ cup	160 milliliters
¾ cup	180 milliliters
1 cup (8 fluid ounces)	240 milliliters
1¼ cups	300 milliliters
1½ cups (12 fluid ounces)	360 milliliters
1¾ cups	400 milliliters
2 cups (1 pint)	460 milliliters
3 cups	700 milliliters
4 cups (1 quart)	0.95 liter
1 quart plus ¼ cup	1 liter
4 quarts (1 gallon)	3.8 liters

WEIGHT

¼ ounce	7 grams
½ ounce	14 grams
¾ ounce	21 grams
1 ounce	28 grams
1¼ ounces	35 grams
1½ ounces	42.5 grams
1⅔ ounces	45 grams
2 ounces	57 grams
3 ounces	85 grams
4 ounces (¼ pound)	113 grams
5 ounces	142 grams
6 ounces	170 grams
7 ounces	198 grams
8 ounces (½ pound)	227 grams
16 ounces (1 pound)	454 grams
35.25 ounces (2.2 pounds)	1 kilogram

LENGTH

⅛ inch	3 millimeters
¼ inch	6 millimeters
½ inch	1.25 centimeters
1 inch	2.5 centimeters
2 inches	5 centimeters
2½ inches	6 centimeters
4 inches	10 centimeters
5 inches	13 centimeters
6 inches	15.25 centimeters
12 inches (1 foot)	30 centimeters

OVEN TEMPERATURES

To convert Fahrenheit to Celsius, subtract 32 from Fahrenheit, multiply the result by 5, then divide by 9.

DESCRIPTION	FAHRENHEIT	CELSIUS	BRITISH GAS MARK
Very cool	200°	95°	0
Very cool	225°	110°	¼
Very cool	250°	120°	½
Cool	275°	135°	1
Cool	300°	150°	2
Warm	325°	165°	3
Moderate	350°	175°	4
Moderately hot	375°	190°	5
Fairly hot	400°	200°	6
Hot	425°	220°	7
Very hot	450°	230°	8
Very hot	475°	245°	9

COMMON INGREDIENTS & THEIR APPROXIMATE EQUIVALENTS

1 cup uncooked white rice = 185 grams

1 cup all-purpose flour = 140 grams

1 stick butter (4 ounces • ½ cup • 8 tablespoons) = 110 grams

1 cup butter (8 ounces • 2 sticks • 16 tablespoons) = 220 grams

1 cup brown sugar, firmly packed = 225 grams

1 cup granulated sugar = 200 grams

Information compiled from a variety of sources, including *Recipes into Type* by Joan Whitman and Dolores Simon (Newton, MA: Biscuit Books, 1993); *The New Food Lover's Companion* by Sharon Tyler Herbst (Hauppauge, NY: Barron's, 2013); and *Rosemary Brown's Big Kitchen Instruction Book* (Kansas City, MO: Andrews McMeel, 1998).

Index

Andrews McMeel Publishing, LLC
an Andrews McMeel Universal company
1130 Walnut Street, Kansas City, Missouri 64106

www.andrewsmcmeel.com

15 16 17 18 19 SHO 10 9 8 7 6 5 4 3 2 1

ISBN: 978-1-4494-7266-5

Library of Congress Control Number: 2015944324

Photographer: Ben Pieper
Images on pages ii, 13, 57, 63, and 80 used under license from Shutterstock.com
Food Stylist: Sarah Jane Hunt
Editor: Jean Lucas
Art Director: Julie Barnes
Illustration: Brenna Thummler
Production Editor: Maureen Sullivan
Production Manager: Carol Coe
Demand Planner: Sue Eikos

ATTENTION: SCHOOLS AND BUSINESSES
Andrews McMeel books are available at quantity discounts with bulk purchase for educational, business, or sales promotional use. For information, please e-mail the Andrews McMeel Publishing Special Sales Department: specialsales@amuniversal.com.